Basics of Singing

FOURTH EDITION

D0146989

Jan Schmidt

Schirmer Books

An Imprint of Simon & Schuster Macmillan
New York

Prentice Hall International
London   Mexico City   New Delhi   Singapore   Sydney   Toronto

Schirmer Books
An Imprint of Simon & Schuster Macmillan
1633 Broadway
New York, New York 10019

Library of Congress Catalog Card Number: 97-31428

Printed in the United States of America

Printing Number
1 2 3 4 5 6 7 8 9 10

Library of Congress Cataloging-in-Publication Data
Schmidt, Jan.
    Basics of singing / Jan Schmidt. — 4th ed.
        p.   cm.
    Includes bibliographical references (p.   ) and index.
    Contents: Technique — Song anthology
    ISBN 0-02-864745-9 (alk. paper)
    1. Singing—Methods.   I. Title.
MT825.B27   1997
783′.043—dc21   97-31428
                                                                                                        CIP
                                                                                                        MN

This paper meets the requirements of ANSI/NISO Z39. 48-1992 (Permanence of Paper).

To those members of my family who have supported
and encouraged my study of music.

To contact Jan Schmidt call
Singers Hotline: **1-900-890-SONG**
Internet: **http://www.cybersong.com**

To order Schirmer Books call
800-257-5157
Internet: **http://www.mlr.com/schirmer**

Contents

Song Anthology Contents

Art Songs and Arias

Preface

This book is intended as a text and song collection for **beginning and intermediate singing** students enrolled in class or individual voice study at the college or university level. To be most helpful, it should be used under the supervision of a competent teacher who will adapt and amplify its contents.

Information in the text is meant to be direct and easily understood. As can be seen in the bibliography, it is compiled from some of the most authoritative sources available. The **new illustrations,** although simplified for clarity of understanding, are anatomically correct.

The **forty-five songs** in the anthology, featuring many new selections for the current edition, are divided into three categories: fifteen from the folk idiom, fifteen from musical theater, and fifteen art songs and arias. The songs are highly appealing to the contemporary student and are valuable as tools for voice building. All songs are printed in keys of comfortable singing ranges. Some songs appear in high and low keys so that a single edition of **this text will serve all voices.**

New to the Fourth Edition is the inclusion of brief historical and performance notes for the songs included in the anthology. The number of vocal exercises in the text has been doubled, and revised and updated entries appear in the For Further Study and Bibliography sections of the book. The current folk song choices reflect a broader scope of ethnic influences than in previous editions, and the theater songs again represent both movie and stage musicals.

Available with the Fourth Edition are practice **tapes and compact disks containing melodies and accompaniments for the songs** presented in the anthology. Although students should strive to play song melodies themselves, it is hoped that the tapes and CDs will assist those who have not yet mastered adequate keyboard skills to accomplish this goal.

Foreign language texts have been recorded before the "High Voice" accompaniment of songs to which they relate. The combination of book and recorded accompaniment affords students the opportunity to individually explore a wide sampling of song literature from several centuries and styles and to understand more clearly how, musically, we arrived at where we are today.

Acknowledgments

Special words of appreciation are offered here for the instruction in voice performance and vocal pedagogy offered by my principal teachers, William Vennard and Robert Bernard, and by my coach, James Low. Thanks also to Kevin Wiley, Jeff Rizzo, and Ray Briggs for their assistance in the selection of art, theater, and folk songs, respectively, to Henrietta Carter and especially to Jean Shackleton for her significant contributions to the anthology and recordings. Information provided by Donald Carroll for Background and Performance Notes is also acknowledged with gratitude.

Like many other teachers, I am grateful for the research and writing of Drs. Van Lawrence, Ingo Titze, and Robert Sataloff. I wish to express appreciation for permission to include some of their work and thank Dr. David Kritz for his suggestions pertaining to Chapter 6, Vocal Health, in this edition.

Exceptional support has been received at every stage in the conception, production, and marketing of this book. To Jill Lectka and the distinguished staff at Schirmer Books, and to the many voice teachers who have used the various editions of this text and submitted valuable suggestions for new editions, I express my deepest thanks.

PART I

Technique

ONE

Practicing

Learning to sing is a slow and patient undertaking, in which a good ear is the prerequisite, the imagery is an aid supplied by the teacher, and the experience is gradually accumulated until it is so powerful that merely calling up the memory will reproduce it.

In his book, *Singing: The Mechanism and the Technic*, William Vennard wrote the foregoing quote, which seems to be as appropriate a statement to consider as any when one begins a formalized study of singing. Perhaps the words "slow," "patient," and "gradually" should be capitalized. At least, they should be stressed in the student's mind, as should be the necessity of faith in the teacher. The teacher will tailor the suggestions made in this or any other text to a student's particular needs, thus rendering it considerably more valuable.

Singing is a learned skill, and all those with sufficient motivation and intelligence can improve their performance considerably if they commit themselves to it. When it is finally learned, singing is a thoroughly comfortable and enjoyable experience. It's more than that—it's exhilarating! But as one first makes an effort at voice training, it is often confusing and sometimes excruciatingly embarrassing, emotions that eventually pass, after enough performances have been sung. Students are asked to make sounds they cannot easily make, and when they are finally assured by the teacher that they are indeed succeeding, they often dislike what they hear, or simply feel that a tone is strange. That is where the patience is required.

The slowness of learning to sing correctly refers to the great amount of experimentation the student needs to do, both under the teacher's supervision and, particularly, in private practice. Improving one's singing is a never-ending project for most professionals and many amateurs. Mastering the basic skills for a "solid" singing tech-

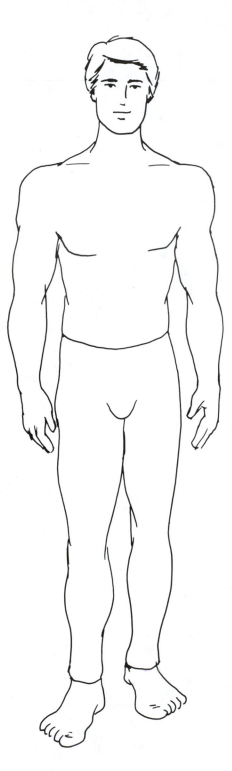

FIGURE 1.1

Correct stance for singing

nique for popular, theater, or classical music takes years, not months. It is similar to learning a new sport, in the sense that the coordination of numerous muscles is involved. Therefore, for some time, students should expect more "misses" than "hits." When one also realizes that techniques for styling and presentation must be learned as well, an understanding of the size of the task begins to develop.

As students continue to work at building their singing voices, they gain a progressively clearer concept of what to expect from themselves. That this concept is aided enormously by the ear is obvious, but students also begin to recognize and memorize the physical sensations they experience when singing correctly. "Singing by feeling" is especially noticeable as they sing in more and more varied circumstances and the acoustics change with each room and situation.

In order to make adequate progress, the singer must practice carefully and consistently. Since, in such areas as lower jaw and throat positions, the student is often dealing with adjustments involving a fraction of an inch, it can readily be seen that concentration must be exclusively on singing. As many distractions as possible must be eliminated. If, at first, concentration does not extend beyond ten minutes, stop practicing! For without concentration, the beginning voice student will slip back into the familiar—and probably incorrect—manner of singing. It is better to do several short, concentrated practice sessions in a day than to do more lengthy, unfocused sessions.

There are numerous approaches to teaching singing, and many can be successful, but most teachers would agree that practicing should be done in a solitary, quiet place, and always in a standing position. This means that practicing while driving from place to place is not particularly helpful to voice building; neither is trying to sing quietly in an apartment or dormitory room. If practice facilities are not available, public buildings with pianos, such as churches, often are. And their proprietors are usually cooperative in letting students use rooms and instruments.

The generally accepted stance for a good singing posture is as follows (see also Figure 1.1).

The feet should be planted firmly on the floor, slightly apart (approximately 12 inches, 300 mm.), one slightly ahead of the other. The weight should be on the forward portion of the feet, to allow greater flexibility in breathing and also to create a more energetic impression when one sings for an audience.

The knees should be slightly bent, to allow the singer to stand as firmly as possible. It often happens that one is inadvertently pushed or bumped during a rehearsal or performance, and, to say nothing of the benefits good posture provides for good voice production, a secure stance is definitely to a singer's advantage.

Shoulders should be firmly back and down, neither tense nor drooping. A differentiation should be made here between this position and the extremely low shoulder position required of dancers.

Arms should hang at the sides in a very relaxed manner, slightly bent at the elbows. This bend creates a less militaristic look than would perfectly straight arms.

The hands of new singing students often tend to express the nervousness they are feeling. Many people, therefore, find it helpful, particularly during lessons, to place the fingertips firmly on the sides of the thighs and to keep them there.

The neck should be relaxed both in front and in back and should not be turned even the slightest degree. Because of unconscious head movement, the neck is frequently stretched in various directions, so special attention should be given to guarding against this. It will prevent straining the muscles from which the voice box is suspended.

The head position should be determined by the focus of the eyes, which should be straight ahead. Being aware that the neck is relaxed will also help to ensure that the head is neither too far back nor too far forward. Generally, the chin should be parallel to the floor.

Essentially, there are four pieces of equipment that are of incalculable assistance to a singer. They are two mirrors, a penlight, and a cassette tape recorder. The mirrors should be of two kinds: one, full length, from which the student can gauge overall posture and appearance, with the second a small hand mirror, with which throat position can be evaluated. The penlight can be shined into the mouth and throat to greatly facilitate the observation with the hand mirror. The tape recorder should be used to make an auditory check on performance progress.

To listen to oneself can be terribly uncomfortable, but there is perhaps no quicker method of correcting a mistake than to hear it when it is played back, and to recognize it as coming from an external source. The recording limitations of the machine cause the voice to sound considerably less sonorous than it actually is, but it is nevertheless a valuable aid to practicing. If students do not have a piano available for use, or do not know how to play one, they can, and should, record vocal exercises and songs given to them by their teacher.

Again, practicing, to progress as quickly as possible, demands absolute concentration and attention to the smallest details. If there is a more efficient or beautiful way to sing a note, stop and try it again. Those with the most to gain from paying attention to details are the singers themselves. If concentration falters, relax for a few minutes, then resume your practicing. A beginning voice student is generally able to practice for thirty minutes, maintaining concentration and exercising the voice, without tiring.

TWO

Vocalizing

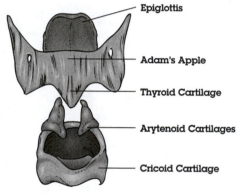

FIGURE 2.1

Front view of the separated cartilages of the larynx

Epiglottis

Adam's Apple

Thyroid Cartilage

Arytenoid Cartilages

Cricoid Cartilage

Every practice session should begin with a period of vocalizing, exercising, or "warming up" the voice. If a student is planning to practice for thirty minutes, for example, half of that time might well be allocated to *vocalises* (vocal exercises) and half to the study of songs. The reasons for vocalizing can be more readily understood when the student realizes that the vocal cords are actually muscles that extend from the front to the back of the throat, and that, in fact, one is learning to coordinate them and the other muscles in the *larynx* (voice box), with the airstream. Vocalises will increase blood circulation, flexibility, and responsiveness, characteristics that can then be transferred to the songs.

Voice students need to understand how the body participates in the singing process. Because this understanding aids in analyzing reasons for desirable and undesirable voice production, some simplified drawings (Figures 2.1–2.4), augmented by discussion, are included here.

Vertically, the adult larynx measures about one and a half inches (40 mm.). The average measurement if its circumference is five inches (125 mm.). At puberty, the male larynx sometimes enlarges more dramatically than does the female, accounting for the difficulty in coordinating the action of the laryngeal muscles often experienced by teenage boys.

The larynx is composed of two major cartilages—*cartilage* being that bodily substance that can develop into bone—namely, the cricoid and the thyroid. The *cricoid* is actually a specialized cartilaginous ring at the upper end of the windpipe. It is shaped like a signet ring, with the signet in the back of the throat and the shaft of the ring in the front of the throat. The *thyroid*, which we frequently identify as the Adam's apple, is V-shaped, with the angle of the V in the front of the throat, and the open portion in the back.

6

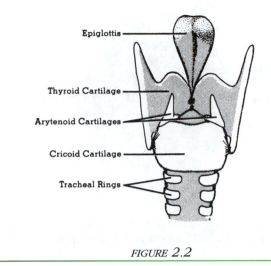

FIGURE 2.2

Back view of the larynx

The *vocal cords*, also called *vocal folds*, attach to the thyroid cartilage in the front, stretch backward across the path of the airstream, and attach to the two small *arytenoids*, pyramid-shaped cartilages, in the back. These small cartilages sit upon the upper edge of the cricoid, gliding along its surface. Because of the action of the laryngeal muscles, these cartilages approach each other and the vocal cords are brought together hundreds of times per second.

There are, in all, five groups of muscles in the larynx, including the vocal cords, or *thyroarytenoids* named for the cartilages to which they attach, and ten cartilages. Only the leaf-shaped epiglottis, readily seen in the drawings, might well be mentioned at this stage of study. It is of particular interest because of its size and shape and because of its function. It lies back across the top of the larynx frequently during swallowing, diverting food particles across the windpipe, into the esophagus.

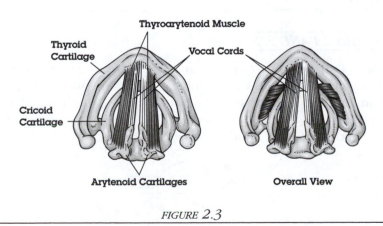

FIGURE 2.3

Top view of the muscles inside the larynx

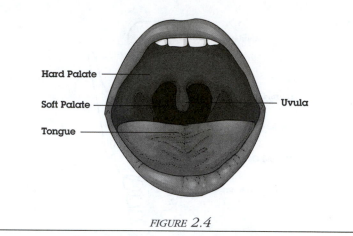

FIGURE 2.4

Front view of open throat position

Now to the practical points of vocalization.

In the following paragraphs, a set of progressive vocalises will be given. The possibility exists for devising literally hundreds of vocal exercises, most of which might be used advantageously. It is important to realize precisely for what reason a vocalise is used. For the beginning student, a fairly set and limited number of exercises might be the preferable regimen. Again, they should be worked on for at least fifteen minutes before proceeding to the practice of songs.

A well-produced sung tone is based on what is often termed an "open" throat. The process for learning this technique can be accelerated by using the *oh* vowel for a period of time instead of the *ah* vowel. The *oh* vowel more quickly enables the singer to get used to an elevated soft palate (the muscular portion of the roof of the mouth, directly behind the hard palate) and the lowered tongue, the two primary indicators of an open throat. It is also true that most new voice students do not stretch open the throat to the extent that they imagine, and the *oh* will counteract this tendency.

Vocalises

EXERCISES 2.1 AND 2.2

Silently yawn the throat open, and at the beginning stage of the yawn, quietly slide from your highest comfortable pitch to your lowest comfortable pitch on the vowel *oh* or *ah*. Using a hand mirror and penlight in this and all succeeding exercises, be certain the tongue and palate remain absolutely still. Repeat.

ah _____

Proceeding in a similar manner, begin a yawn, quietly slide from your lowest comfortable pitch to your highest comfortable pitch, then back down to your lowest comfortable pitch.

Goal: To maintain a constantly high palate and lowered tongue and an even, unbroken tone.

Avoid: The arching tongue, lowering palate, and breaks in the tone. If breaks should occur, add a little nasality to the vowel by temporarily using the syllable "honk." Be careful not to use the full part of the yawn, or the throat will be too widely opened, resulting in a depressed tongue and "gagging" sensation.

EXERCISES 2.3–2.6

Using the same method required in the first vocalises, and proceeding in this and all vocalises upward by half steps, slide between pitches of a perfect fifth on the *oh* or *ah* vowel. All exercises should be developed to as high a pitch as is comfortable; then descend by half steps back to the original starting pitch. This arrangement is used because the vocal cords ar more relaxed on low pitches than they are on high ones.

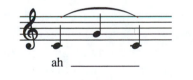

> *Goal:* Same as Exercises 2.1 and 2.2
>
> *Avoid:* Same as Exercises 2.1 and 2.2

EXERCISES 2.7 AND 2.8

Retaining the "open" throat on the *oh* or *ah* vowel, and sliding between pitches, sing the following pitches.

    Goal: Same as exercises 2.1 to 2.6. Also listen for a consistent, unchanging vowel throughout the range of the vocalise.

    Avoid: The same undesirable characteristics mentioned for exercises 2.1 to 2.7. Be careful to eliminate *h*'s between notes, by paying more attention to sliding.

EXERCISES 2.9–2.11

Using the same directions given for Exercise 2.3, slide through octaves. Introducing a very slight nasal quality by thinking the syllable *on*, as in "honk," into the vowel in the extreme high and low pitches will facilitate the singing of this vocalise.

Goal: To maintain a constant vowel, uninterrupted tone, and consistent volume level throughout the range of each exercise. These exercises are also helpful in developing a wider singing range.

Avoid: The changing vowel, *h's*, and lowering volume between pitches.

EXERCISE 2.12

To clarify more fully the tongue positions required for the different vowels, sing the following vowel series on a single pitch. The vowels should be sung with low jaw and high palate and should seem to "melt" into one another. The tip of the tongue should be in approximately the same place for the *ee* and *ay* vowels. For most students, "head tone," a vibration in the head, should be felt in the same place as the vowels progress.

ee   ay   ah   oh   oo

Goal: Same as Exercise 2.6.

Avoid: Same as Exercise 2.6.

EXERCISE 2.13

To assist in accelerating the airflow, sing the following exercise, teeth apart, lower lip lightly touching upper teeth for the initial *vee* sound. Conceive of the pitches as sweeping upward instead of lowering, so that the airflow will continue to move energetically.

vee _____   vee _____   vee _____   vee

Goal: To transcend the "breathy" phase of voice production until a brilliant "core" is consistently sung into the tone. It will often result in "head tone" and "ringing in the ears."

Avoid: Singing with clenched teeth and a fluctuating amount of brilliance.

THREE

Breathing

As soon as the principle of the open throat has been clearly understood and somewhat integrated into the vocalises, the basics of good breath support, perhaps the most important single element in the production of beautiful tone, should be reviewed. The open throat was discussed first, because, when blown against a tight throat, an energetic airstream, regardless of its amount of control, can create discomfort and hoarseness.

Beginning with the physiological process of breathing (see Figure 3.1), the windpipe, or *trachea*, is made up of a series of cartilaginous rings somewhat resembling a vacuum hose. It is about four and a half inches (114 mm.) long, with an average diameter of three-quarters of an inch (19 mm.). Connecting the rings are muscle and membrane. The same membranous tissue also covers the larynx, throat, mouth, and nose—important information when considering the effects of upper-respiratory infections. The trachea eventually subdivides into two *bronchi*, one bronchus for each lung. The bronchi further subdivide into numerous *bronchioles*, through which oxygen passes into the lungs.

The *lungs* are made of spongy membranous tissue, which is formed into two sacs, one located in the right side of the chest, the other in the left. Oxygen passes through these membranes into the blood. The lungs also dispose of certain waste products, such as carbon dioxide. They can expand their capacity only as far as the ribs will allow, which is one reason why it is important for singers to keep the position of the ribs raised and out. In a cycle of deep inhalation and exhalation, such as that used in singing, three and a half quarts (3.3 liters) of air may be exhaled, leaving one and a half quarts (1.4 liters) of residual air in the lungs. Because new singing students often mistakenly operate on the premise of "saving air"

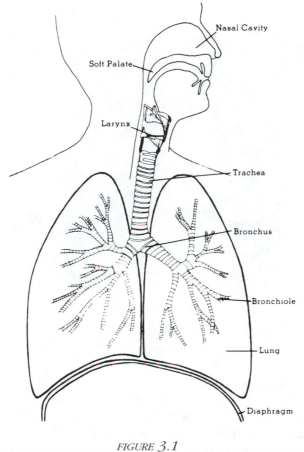

Nasal Cavity

Soft Palate

Larynx

Trachea

Bronchus

Bronchiole

Lung

Diaphragm

FIGURE 3.1

Respiratory system

while they sing, it is important to be aware of the large quantity of air that can and should be used.

Assisting in the raising and lowering of the ribs are the *intercostal* muscles (see Figure 3.2). The backward and downward position of the shoulders also enables the ribs to be positioned most optimally for maximum lung expansion. The ribs should be maintained in this expanded condition during exhalation as well as inhalation, in order to prevent their weight prematurely pushing air out of the lungs.

Below the lungs lies the *diaphragm*. It is a massive, dome-shaped muscle, which divides the chest cavity from the abdominal cavity (see Figure 3.1). It attaches to the lower ribs and vertebrae, with its dome pointing up toward the chest cavity. It is the most important muscle of inhalation. As one inhales, the diaphragm, flattens, allowing the lungs to inflate. One consequence of this action is that—and singers should take careful note of it—during inhalation, the abdominal muscles will move outward as the abdominal contents are compressed by the lowering of the diaphragm. Conversely, at

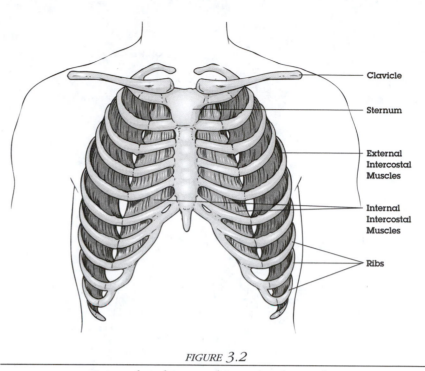

Clavicle

Sternum

External
Intercostal
Muscles

Internal
Intercostal
Muscles

Ribs

FIGURE 3.2

Internal and external intercostal muscles

exhalation, which occurs while a tone is being produced, the general direction of the abdominal muscles will usually be movement inward (see Figure 3.3). Most new voice students move their abdominal muscles in exactly the opposite direction from that which is ideal.

As the muscles of the chest are most active at inhalation, so the muscles of the abdomen are most active at exhalation. There are four groups of abdominal muscles, all of which are called into action during singing. As can be seen in Figure 3.4, the area covered by the abdominals extends from the *sternum* (breastbone) and ribs to the pubic bone and around to the back. It is important that they be relaxed during inhalation throughout their total expanse, to allow maximum intake of air.

For an even release of air, the singer may influence diaphragmatic movement by flexible and smooth contraction of the abdominals during exhalation. Although it is typical of "well-supported" singing to feel muscular exertion in the back, a new student might pull in the abdominal muscles too rapidly, resulting in discomfort. To avoid this occurrence and to keep the pressure of the rising abdomen off the diaphragm for as long as possible, the singer should be certain that inward abdominal movement is paced with the musical phrase. It should be slow and gradual unless an increased amount of air is needed to produce a higher or louder pitch. When this situation occurs, the rising diaphragm will push air out of the lungs with more force if the abdominals are pulled in more quickly.

Now that the mechanics of breathing have been discussed, the voice-building process will be helped by reviewing the vocalises listed in Chapter 2 with an expanded view of their purpose. In addi-

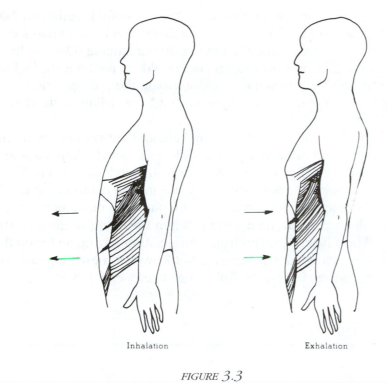

Inhalation   Exhalation

FIGURE 3.3

Muscle action during breathing

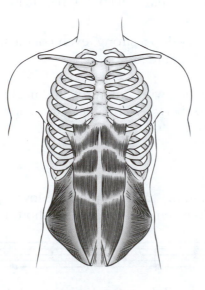

FIGURE 3.4

Muscles of the abdomen

tion to the concentration on the open throat, careful breathing habits should be observed. That is, the abdominals should be expanded at inhalation and move gradually inward during singing. Once exhalation is begun, the inward movement should be continuous, including the "spaces" between the notes. Stopping the pulling action after each pitch results in a "punchy-sounding" vocal line, instead of a smooth one.

The ribs should be kept in an upward and outward position during inhalation and exhalation. The shoulders should be kept back and down, never moving, during inhalation and exhalation. Finally, a check can be made on this process, by placing the palms of the hands on the abdomen, fingers spread, to monitor the movement of the abdominals throughout their length. When breathing is efficient, the result will be a flexible, uninterrupted tone. After having reviewed the vocalises in Chapter 2 (Exercises 2.1–2.7) with a new emphasis on breathing, concentrate on the following (Exercises 3.1–3.5).

Vocalises

EXERCISE 3.1

At the rate of one exhalation per second, and using the *hoh* or *hah* syllable, speak the sounds while rapidly pulling in the abdominal muscles. It is important to allow the abdominals to relax (move outward) after each syllable.

hah		hah		hah		hah	
(in)	(out)	(in)	(out)	(in)	(out)	(in)	(out)

Goal: To develop a strong, even contraction of the abdominal muscles over their entire area.

Avoid: Singing with a high jaw and neglecting to allow the abdominals to relax between syllables (the consequence of which is muscular spasm).

EXERCISE 3.2

Using the "open throat" and keeping the lower jaw down and back, sing the arpeggio given, on *staccato*, or short, notes.

hah   hah   hah   hah   hah

Goal: To add facility to the pattern of abdominal movement established in the vocalise in Exercise 3.1.

Avoid: Same difficulties discussed in Exercise 3.1.

EXERCISES 3.3–3.6

For greater flexibility, sing the following pattern using the *oh* or *ah* vowel with an unbroken (*legato*) line of absolutely consistent quality. Use the concept of sliding pitch to pitch. Add very slight nasality on the upper and lower tones for greater ease of performance and to give more fullness to sound. The first pitch in each group of three (marked with the horizontal "v" [>]) of three should be slightly accented, by rapidly contracting, then relaxing, the abdominal muscles. For exercises with consonants, the teeth should always be kept apart, with only the tongue and lips adjusted to create the sounds.

Goal: To coordinate the activity of the abdominal muscles with the airflow, resulting in a flexible, smooth line.

Avoid: Fluctuating volume level and interrupted flow of tone.

EXERCISES 3.7-3.8

To develop volume, sustain these exercises for sixteen beats, at a moderate tempo, using the *oh* or *ah* vowel. Gradually increase the volume to the loudest comfortable level, then gradually decrease to the original level, always pulling inward on the abdominals. Blow out air more rapidly as volume builds.

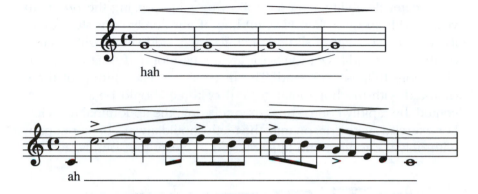

hah _____

ah _____

Goal: To fluctuate volume levels, using an unbroken line and an evenly distributed progression of sound.

Avoid: Sacrificing tone as the volume level is altered because of a changing vowel or an erratic vibrato.

EXERCISES 3.9

Repeat exercise 2.1 to relax cords.

ah _____

FOUR

Learning a Song

To transfer good technique from vocalises to songs is a primary goal of singers at all stages of development. Just as practicing should always and without exception begin with concentration on technique in the vocalises, so, then, should careful thought be given to ways of transferring that same technique to songs, whether those songs are classical, theater, or pop. Although there are different types of techniques for various songs, exercises covered in the first year or two of voice study are usually so general that even the most dedicated pop singers will not damage their commercial potential by using them.

The emphasis in transferring technique to songs is not directed, necessarily, toward allowing the singer finally to sound "natural." The emphasis is rather on vocal health, beauty of tone, and effective musical interpretation. Singing "naturally" is almost never good enough. Performers whose technique give that illusion have generally spent thousands of solitary hours thinking and practicing to improve their performance.

The frequent impression of new voice students is that the incorporation of technique into their songs gives them too much of an operatic sound. Another impression often mentioned is that a song is too high. Because we usually speak with the mouth nearly closed, it seems strange to open it for a more sonorous tone during singing. This fuller sound, which is often thought of by the new student as "too classical," is actually the first step toward beautiful singing and can be heard in good performers working in all styles.

It is also a source of amazement to many to hear themselves producing greater volume and singing on a higher pitch or with a different quality than that to which they have been accustomed all their lives. Learning to sing songs that at first seem too high develops greater breath control and strengthens the vocal muscles. It extends the singer's options when selecting material to perform, enlarges the possibilities for styling, and, quite basically, improves the entire range of the voice.

As with practicing vocalises, the tape recorder is an indispensable aid to learning a song. The singer may have the melody line first taped without, then with, the piano accompaniment, in order to expedite the learning process. The audio tapes and compact disks available with this book offer accompaniments with prominently featured melody lines for songs included in the anthology. As the learning of the song progresses, the singing should periodically be recorded, played back, and carefully analyzed. The teacher's guidance in assessing the technique used in the song and its interpretation is vital, since it is extremely difficult for singers to evaluate themselves. But it is the students who will ultimately decide the extent of their own success. As with vocalizing, the successful singer will be the one who follows directions given, in the most minute detail, and who practices consistently with enormous concentration.

The order of the steps for learning a song varies according to the learning patterns of a singer. The following approach is but one workable method. To help illustrate the steps, an art song from the anthology, "Beneath a Weeping Willow's Shade," will be used. The assumption is made that any song studied has been approved for the student's use by the teacher.

To begin, record the melody on the tape recorder, first without the accompaniment, then with the complete piano part. Play the recording of the unaccompanied melody once, then repeat if desired, silently following along with the music.

Next, play the melody with accompaniment. Notice the general feeling of the music, whether, for example, it is heavy or descriptive (with an accent every two beats, like a march, or every three beats like a waltz). Check the dates of the composer to find out if the song is fairly recent or from some other period. By considering the text and music, determine the overall style of the song. Was it intended to be a folk song, a song for worship, for the theater, or for some other use entirely?

"Beneath a Weeping Willow's Shade" (see Exercise 4.1) was written during the lifetime of George Washington; therefore, the picture of men and women in the dress of that time dancing to the music of the harpsichord might readily be imagined. The feeling is light and buoyant, with an accent on every third beat.

Return in the music to the unaccompanied melody and, using the syllable *la*, sing along, being careful that the sung pitches and rhythms are exactly the same as those heard on the piano. This step should be repeated as many times as necessary to accomplish this goal. One time-saving device is to isolate those places in the melody that are repeatedly sung incorrectly or are in any way difficult. Above them, mark an *x* with pencil which can later be erased as they are mastered. In "Beneath a Weeping Willow's Shade," measures 8, 9, and 35 might be confusing because of the dotted rhythms (notes with dots following are held half again longer than they would be normally, resulting in the shortening of the note that follows). Measures 25 and 26 might prove surprising because of the introduction of wider intervals between the notes of the melody (until that point, most of the notes have been adjacent to one another in the scale, or very nearly so).

When the pitches and rhythms are learned, whisper the words of the text in rhythm while playing back the unaccompanied melody. This could well be done two or three times, or until there are no difficulties performing this step. In all songs, a word is found directly underneath the note to which it corresponds. Frequently, two or more notes are sung on the same syllable. In measure 8, "wil" is sung on two notes, and in measure 32 "way" is sung on seven notes.

After the music and text have been put together, some time should be taken to analyze and picture the meaning and mood of the text. Read the text aloud. What exactly is the text trying to communicate? Then, with pencil, mark a comma in each place where a breath seems sensible, taking into consideration the sound of the melody and the meaning of the words. Breaths are taken to separate thoughts. For example, in measure 12, a breath separates "Her hand upon her heart she laid" from "And plaintive was her moan." And in measure 4, second verse, a breath separates "Fond Echo to her strains replied" from "The winds her sorrow bore." Sections of repeated text, such as those found in measure 28, are also usually separated with a breath.

Another necessity, in order to effectively give expression to a text, is to research the meaning of any words not understood. In "Beneath a Weeping Willow's Shade," measure 3, second verse, Echo (the nymph from Greek mythology who faded away for love of Narcissus, retaining only her voice) is mentioned. And in measure 27, the word *dulcet* (meaning "melodious") is used. In foreign-language songs, every word must be clearly understood by the singer, a process that is simplified as more and more foreign-language songs are learned. Knowing the "general meaning" is never enough.

After the music and text are memorized, attention should be turned once again to technique and its transference to the song. The correctness of the breathing should be checked. Are the abdominals moving out at inhalation? Are the ribs maintained in an upward and outward position? Are the shoulders still and in the proper position?

And what about good articulation?

Strange as it feels, the essence of good articulation is to sing with the upper and lower teeth apart, using a flexible tongue and lips to form the words. This combination coupled with a constantly elevated soft palate allows for more vertical space inside the mouth, which prevents the sound from being unduly dampened by its soft structures.

Piano acc. adapted
from the original by
Roy S. Stoughton

Beneath a Weeping Willow's Shade

Words and Music
by Francis
Hopkinson
(1737–1791)

Dedicated to George Washington, Esquire

plain - tive was her moan, And plain - tive was her moan.

ne'er shall see thee more, I ne'er shall see thee more."

The mock - bird sat up - on a bough, The

mock - bird sat up - on a bough And lis - ten'd to her lay, Then to the dis - tant

Depending on the type of tone quality a teacher might prefer, one abbreviated pronunciation guide for new students might be the following:

Vernacular	International Phonetic Alphabet	Guide
ee	[i]	Pronounced as the vowel sound in "feet," using low jaw, high palate, tongue and lips forward.
ay	[e]	A diphthong which begins like the vowel sound in "pet" and, at its release, concludes in the position for an *it*, as in "it," with no movement of the lowered jaw between sounds.
ah	[a]	The vowel in "palm," with the same low jaw position used for *ee* and *ay*.
oh	[o]	The position of the palate for this sound is high. Heard in "tone," this sound uses a jaw position that is somewhat lower than for the preceding vowels with the palate raised.
oo	[u]	The vowel sound heard in "moon," pronounced with lips forward and the jaw in the low position used for *oh*. The palate will be as highly arched as possible.

Vowels should be modified from the foregoing guide in words that require it, so that pronunciation of texts is perceived as natural. For example, the vowel in the first syllable of "willow" will be pronounced in a way that more closely resembles its spoken pronunciation than it does "*wee*llow."

In good articulation, a tone quality should be continuous throughout the phrase. This means that the character of the tone should not fluctuate between shrill and hooty as syllables change.

Consonants, because they dissipate more rapidly than vowels, must be emphasized more heavily in singing than in speech. Otherwise, the meaning of a text will be totally lost even in a small auditorium.

When a song has been thoroughly worked through, first musically, then technically, it is time to consider how to communicate it. Videotape is a great help when working to improve this area. Practicing before a full-length mirror is a useful alternative. The singer needs, quite literally, to picture the things being sung about. Concentration, which must also be practiced, is the key.

If a performer identifies strongly enough with the text of a song, actually picturing himself in a place, a situation, or as a certain person, that is all he will be able to think about. The term "acting" is often misinterpreted. "Being," not "acting," is what touches audiences.

Simultaneously, the music must be sung effectively, shaped by the demands of the composer and the emotions of the singer. And, of course, the audience must be drawn in—convinced—that the singer is exactly who he presumes to be and feels exactly what he proclaims to feel. It is a heady task, and, when everything is synchronous, the highest of "highs."

Songs must be delivered with great energy to an audience. New singers often feel they are almost yelling when they are singing at a volume level acceptable to a teacher. To effectively convince an audience takes double or triple the amount of energy one would imagine. If a student occasionally overdoes it, the teacher will be the first to say so. Even through piano introductions and interludes, the singer's thoughts must center on the mood and content of the song. If one lapses, even momentarily, dramatic intensity will be lost. In the beginning stages, when the transference of technique is often awkward, it is frequently difficult to maintain energy and concentration. But in time, this will come, enabling a singer actually to "sell" a song.

Sample Song-Learning Method

Record melody, first with, then without, accompaniment. Develop familiarity with both versions.

Define the historical period, mood, and type of song.

Sing along with unaccompanied melody using the syllable *la*, marking difficult places with an *x*. Practice until rhythm and pitches are absolutely accurate.

Whisper the words of the text in rhythm while listening to the unaccompanied melody.

Sing text and pitches with unaccompanied melody until learned securely. Sing with accompanied melody.

Read the text aloud and analyze its meaning.

With commas, mark appropriate breaths. Circle expression markings.

Concentrate on the use of good vocal technique in the song.

Using a tape recorder, review articulation.

Practice "selling" the song by picturing its text and performing it with great and consistent energy.

When applying this method to a song in a style different from that of an art song—for example, "How Could I Ever Know?" from musical theater—exactly the same procedure can be used. The biggest difference will be in the mood and styling of the song. The mood of "Beneath a Weeping Willow's Shade," composed in the eighteenth century, is mournful, and intended for private, rather than highly commercial, entertainment. Vocally, an eighteenth-century art song is performed in a very prescribed manner, with continuous vibrato and carefully defined dynamics, which must be meticulously observed.

"How Could I Ever Know?," on the other hand, was composed fairly recently, with a reflective text, and is part of a larger musical theater work, *The Secret Garden.* In musical theater pieces, the singer has an opportunity for more variety of styling, as long as what one does is closely related to the composer's indications in the music. Often, the singing will be more speechlike, meaning that more "straight" tone, using little or no vibrato, is employed. To intelligently interpret a musical theater song or operatic aria, the entire story and other music from the show or opera must be studied, in order to understand how the character might sing the song. This can be done by borrowing recordings and scores from the library.

A folk song, such as "The Juniper Tree" (see page 98), may be from anywhere and any period. This song is from England; its original date of composition unknown. It is quietly clever, and is most attractive when sung with almost continuous vibrato. Because of their casual nature and because frequently they were not originally written out, most folk songs have been reworked countless times. They can be sung with any vocal quality necessary to communicate the spirit of their text, from lyrical to bawdy. The singer should have a consistent enough vocal technique that vocal effects for folk songs, dynamic in presentation and harmless to the voice, can be consciously devised. This same ideal should be the ultimate goal of singers in all types of vocal music performance.

FIVE

Basic Principles of Vocal Technique

I n order to explain more completely the reasoning behind the singing process, some additional information, particularly that related to articulation and acoustics, will be given in this chapter. While much of the information is based on scientific research, some is based on pedagogical experience, a combination of sources common to all teachers. When a process is thoroughly understood, its outcome tends to be more effective, and therefore meaningful. Undesirable effects can be analyzed and avoided, while desirable ones can be incorporated and utilized.

Ideas about articulation vary greatly from teacher to teacher. At one end of the spectrum are those who ask the students for an extremely pulled-down larynx and a deep yawning quality in the tone. At the other are those who speak often of closing the mouth and lifting the muscles in the upper part of the cheeks for a smiling, bright quality. Because the tone quality a teacher elects to teach is so evidently a matter of personal choice, it is important that students be aware of the options open to them when they are in the process of selecting an instructor.

Taking some elements from both extremes of the spectrum can produce a method of articulation that is vocally comfortable and healthy and clearly understandable to listeners.

As the singer begins to transfer technique to songs, it is important to realize that, as one maintains the jaw in a slightly lowered position, so that upper and lower teeth can be kept apart, the throat should be kept open, as it was for the vocalises. The stretching open of the throat might feel exaggerated at first, but it should not feel uncomfortable. Both a throat that is too closed and one that is too widely stretched will produce a feeling of tension in the front of the neck just under the lower jaw. It is imperative to sing with a relaxed neck, since constricting its muscles, in front or back, can pull the cartilages of the larynx into positions that will put unnecessary strain on the vocal cords. Singing with a tight neck is one of the major problems with which beginning voice students must be concerned. It distorts articulation, impairs quality, and markedly limits the number of pitches that can be sung. Often, its most obvious manifestation is a sore throat.

Working from the inside out, when the singer begins to concentrate on opening the throat, a phenomenon similar to yawning, it will be noticed that several things happen. Most obviously, the jaw drops, giving a stretching feeling to the chewing muscles. Simultaneously, the soft palate arches and the tongue lowers. These characteristics should always be maintained while singing a song. A tight jaw or tongue that is too high or too far forward will render articulation less distinguishable, by introducing the *uh* vowel into words intended to project an *ah* sound. Since the soft palate also serves as the floor of the nasal cavity, a lowered soft palate will contribute to the production of a tone with nasal quality. (The slight amount of nasality previously suggested for the extreme high and low pitches of the vocalises will not be counterproductive.) Another important function of the raised palate is that, because of its firm surface, it appears to promote clarity, or give "focus," to the tone. A combination of arched palate and accelerated airflow greatly enhances a tone's carrying power.

Working from the outside inward, when the singer elevates the muscles in the upper part of the cheeks, the upper lip is raised, thus exposing more of the hard surfaces of the teeth. This will contribute to the production of brilliant tone, but it should not be substituted for energetic airflow and arched palate. Because the upper cheeks are elevated, it does not stand to reason that a broad smile should necessarily result. If the text indicates that such an expression would be appropriate, the singer should follow that suggestion. But often a text will imply a more serious expression, for which the lips should be more relaxed.

As singers inhale, they prepare mentally for what they are about to sing. They think of the syllable they will be producing, and thereby assist in the physical, as well as mental, preparation of the body for that syllable.

The *attack*, or beginning of the tone, should feel comfortable and should be neither too explosive nor too breathy. In an explosive attack, the airstream forces the vocal cords apart, and they slap back together again with more force than is vocally healthy or audibly pleasing. In that instance, a popping sound will precede the syllable. In a breathy attack, when a slight rush of air precedes or accompanies the syllable, the cords do not close firmly enough, and air, which could be more efficiently used, is wasted. Consequently, if a singer makes an explosive attack, it is necessary to relax the neck muscles and slow the rate at which one is contracting the abdominals and blowing air. If the attack is breathy, the airflow needs to be accelerated, by pulling in more rapidly on the abdominals and blowing harder.

Smoking is another common cause of breathy production. In the person who smokes, the membranes covering the cords are filled with fluid. Instead of healthy cords opening and closing hundreds of times per second to release clearly defined vibrations, the fluid-filled membranes approximate each other with a closure that is anything but firm. If smoking is stopped, there should be a marked improvement in the clarity of the voice within two weeks.

Following an efficient inhalation and attack, the singer thinks of the totality of the line being sung. To avoid a choppy, word-by-word interpretation of the text, one needs to concentrate on sustaining the vowels of each syllable for as long as it is rhythmically correct to do so. At times it is also helpful to think to the end of the line, keeping part of the concentration on the end of the line of text. These procedures aid greatly in the singing of the *legato*, or smooth, line, one of the prime objectives of advanced singers.

The following are some of the most basic points of correct articulation with which the singer should be familiar:

For the sake of tone quality, the *uh* and *ow* sounds are always altered to an *ah*. This practice is applicable to such words as "love," "the," and "down." Modification of this basic vowel should be used when needed, especially for dipthongs.

Vowels should be clear and brilliant. *Ee*, as in "see," *eh*, as in "when," and *ay,* as in "say," are all pronounced as an *ee*, with lowered jaw and using only the slightest modification.

When *diphthongs*, compound vowels, are sung, the first sound is sustained, with the second sound added at the release of the syllable. For example, in the *a* of "shade," the opening vowel sound *eh* (e) is the sustained sound. The *a* concludes with an *ih* (i) sound, which is added immediately preceding the *d* of "shade" (for example, sheh-ihd). Some other common diphthongs are heard in the words "eye," "poi," and the aforementioned "down," in which the sustained *ah* (a) sound concludes on an *oo* (u).

Consonants are always formed using the tongue and lips, with space between the upper and lower teeth.

When two or more notes are sung on the same syllable, the singer should slide between them. Articulating each of the notes with an *h*, a very common approach, requires that, for each *h*, the airflow be stopped. This, in turn, interrupts the legato line. (Sliding on a run differs from scooping up to a pitch on an attack, which should be avoided.)

The addition of an extra syllable to the end of a word, such as "friend-*uh*," is indicative of overemphasis, and should be avoided.

Linking the final consonant of one word to the initial sound of the following word, when it changes the meaning of the text, should be avoided. An often-cited example of this is, "I'm old."

Good articulation should leave the neck free from tension and be unobtrusive yet render a text clearly understandable.

The measure of effective articulation lies in the quality of its perception. If words cannot be heard, or if a clear understanding of them is difficult for an audience, much of the emotional and intellectual impact of the song is lost. For that reason, some basic information concerning *acoustics*, the study of sound, will be presented.

As the highly flexible vocal cords stretch across the top of the trachea, they open and close in a wavelike motion, from bottom to top. This action divides the exhaled airstream into numerous tiny puffs, or wave fronts, every second. If, for example, they open and close 440 times in a second, the buzz they produce will be perceived as the first A above middle C.

As the wave fronts are emitted, billions of molecules of air are pushed outward in all directions from the source. The moving molecules do not experience a permanent displacement; after the wave passes by, they return to their original position (see Figure 5.1). The moving outward of the molecules is termed *compression*, and the return of the molecules to their original position is called *rarefaction*.

Sound travels at the rate of approximately eleven hundred feet (335 m.) per second. It enters the outer ear and travels through the tubular canal, which is approximately one inch (25 mm.) long. At the end of the ear canal is the sensitive membranous *eardrum*, which vibrates at the same frequency with which it is disturbed by the compressed air molecules (see Figure 5.2).

The motion of the eardrum activates three small bones called *ossicles*, which are suspended in the *middle ear*—a cavity in the skull. Their movement sets up a vibration in the *oval window*, an oval membrane in the wall of the cochlea. The *cochlea*, a spiral bone in the *inner ear*, is filled with fluid. Nerve endings, which transmit vibrating movement to the brain, are also found in the cochlea.

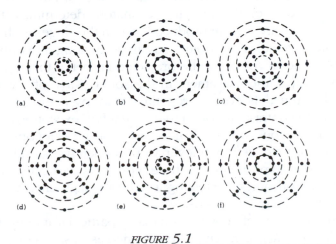

FIGURE 5.1

Traveling pattern of sound waves through air

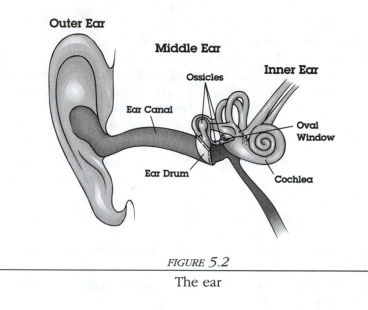

FIGURE 5.2

The ear

Resonance is a response to a produced sound, during which that sound is prolonged and intensified. The three primary resonators for the voice are, in order of importance, the throat, the mouth, and the nose. Research has shown that, although a singer might feel sympathetic vibrations in the chest, trachea, larynx, or sinuses, those areas have little or no value as resonators. When the surfaces of the resonators are stretched to form a yawn or open throat, they are hardened, thereby conducting sound more effectively. The resonators also filter out, or dampen, some sounds, a process that is even more evident when their surfaces are flaccid.

It should be noted that the nose is an occasional resonator, while the throat and mouth function constantly as resonators. Nasal resonance is primarily necessary for the production of nasal consonants, such as *m*, *n*, and *ng*. It is also important in the singing of foreign languages, notably French, because of their nasal vowels.

The shape of the primary resonators determines, to a large extent, the quality of tone produced. When the singer wishes to communicate a vowel, it is usually sustained as long as is rhythmically possible, since a vowel can be projected far better than a consonant. This is because the movement in the sound wave of a vowel, categorized a "tone," is even or repetitive and, by nature, has a longer duration. In contrast, although there are a few exceptions, such as *m* and *n*, most consonants fall into the acoustic category of "noise," which is characterized by uneven or nonrepetitive sound waves (see Figure 5.3). The properties of these types of waves cause their vibrations to fall off quickly, creating a need for high-energy pronunciation of these kinds of sounds.

Another area of acoustics that is of particular interest to singers is registration. *Registers* have been defined as "a series of consecutive similar vocal tones which the musically trained ear can differentiate

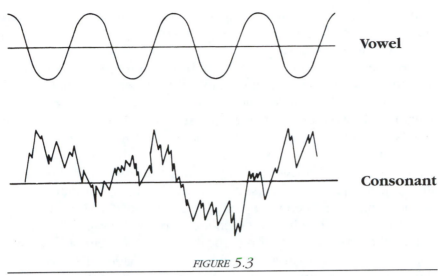

Vowel

Consonant

FIGURE 5.3

Repetitive and nonrepetitive sound waves

at specific places from another adjoining series of likewise internally similar tones."*

Pitch-wise, registers are often referred to by beginning singing students as "low voice," "regular voice," or "high voice." In terms of volume, they are sometimes differentiated by the terms "heavy voice" and "light voice." Regardless of the names applied to registers, most teachers would probably agree that the goal of the student should be to eliminate awareness of their existence. If a singer has "breaks" in the voice and changes in tone quality (vowel color)

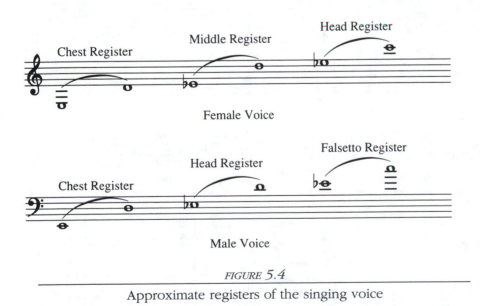

FIGURE 5.4

Approximate registers of the singing voice

* M. Nadoleczny, *Untersuchungen über den Kunstgesang* (Berlin: Springer, 1923).

between high and low pitches, it is simply because that student has not yet learned to coordinate airflow with the actions of the laryngeal musculature and resonators.

Generally, researchers refer to three main registers: *chest, middle,* and *head* in the female voice, and *chest, head,* and *falsetto* in the male voice. In the trained voice, each register is about an octave in length, with several notes that can be sung in either register at those points where the registers overlap (see Figure 5.4).

In nearly all untrained singers, one of the registers, frequently chest, will be used considerably more than the others. It is the task of the student to practice exercising the voice throughout its entire range, so that songs might be interpreted with greater style and beauty.

In those areas where registers overlap, the register is used that makes the most dramatic or musical sense. For example, when a soprano sings "Beneath a Weeping Willow's Shade" (Example 5.1), the word "alone" in measures 5 and 6 could technically be sung in either chest or middle register, but since the text surrounding it is sung in middle register, it is desirable to utilize the same for this word.

EXAMPLE 5.1

SIX

Vocal Health

A healthy voice is fundamental to every singer's ability to communicate effectively. Situations adverse to vocal health occur so frequently that they are often overlooked, resulting in unexpected and sometimes irreversible voice damage.

In an extraordinary and easy-to-understand collection of articles on the subject, Drs. Van Lawrence, Robert Sataloff, Ingo Titze et al. have discussed numerous vocal conditions and how to treat them (see Bibliography). It is with reliance on their respected work and wisdom that the information in this chapter is presented as a general guideline for singers. All specific medical questions should be referred to a physician for responsible diagnosis and treatment, and all directions affixed to medication containers should be read and followed exactly. Complex vocal problems can occasionally involve the integration of several disciplines of medical and dental science. If a vocal problem seems slow to resolve or requires the efforts of several specialists, it is usually helpful to involve a managing physician versed in evaluating and treating disorders in overlapping areas of anatomy and function.

The importance to each person of understanding how his body works, knowing its parts and identifying its idiosyncrasies, goes without saying. It is also vital to understand the side effects of administered medication, relative not only to voice production, but to overall bodily function as well.

Aspirin, perhaps the most common of all medication, is found in many brands of pain medicine and is often ingested by desperate "cold" sufferers. It is contained in Contac, Coricidon, Bufferin, Excedrin, Empirin, Ascripton, and many other remedies for upper respiratory infections. Although it is renowned for its positive effect as a pain reliever, it is almost equally well-known for its use as a blood thinner. Its frequent consumption can increase the possibility of bleeding in the vocal folds, a particular danger in circumstances during which they are in heavy use or when poor vocal technique is being practiced.

Potentially, *anti-inflammatory* medicines containing *ibuprofen,* such as Motrin, Advil, Naprosyn, Aleve, and Indocin, can present the same problem. Sudden loss of voice or slow, progressive loss of range or vocal quality mandates an immediate examination by a laryngologist experienced in treating singers' problems. These are symptoms which may indicate vocal fold hemorrhage. Prompt treatment and on-going follow-up are critical in avoiding permanent changes in voice quality secondary to scar formation.

All anti-inflammatory medications bring side effects. Too high a dose of this class of medicine can sometimes cause stuffiness and a high-pitched noise or ringing in the ears, known as *tinnitus,* and may be caused by aspirin, ibuprofen, steroids, or disorders of the ear. It is also commonly a result of exposure to repeated or intense noises. If this problem occurs, contact a physician immediately. While some cases are reversible, others have a lingering impact. Steps to avoid tinnitus should be carefully followed, and side effects of medication should be discussed in detail with the prescribing physician.

The most effective treatments for the common cold are to drink plenty of liquids, stay in as humid an environment as possible (using a humidifier when necessary), and rest. Saline nose drops or spray such as Afrin and Neo-Synephrine can be used for a period of no more than three or four days, and plain Robitussin can be taken to thin mucous, often reducing the amount of hoarseness and coughing.

Decongestants, which shrink the mucosal lining covering the nose and throat, are often wisely recommended for a cold or stuffy nose. One brand, Sudafed, is frequently suggested for treatment of these conditions. While generally effective, a decongestant can be dangerous to patients with high blood pressure due to their adrenaline-like side effects and can cause sleep deprivation, a major annoyance prior to performance. Tachycardia, or a rapid heart rate, is another frequently reported adverse effect of this class of medication.

Antihistamines, taken for allergic reactions such as sneezing, itchy eyes, and watering nose, are found in many cold remedies and are readily available. While they are effective as relievers of allergic symptoms, some are sedative and dry the mucous membranes. Since singing, particularly during performance, requires fast reflexes and dry vocal folds rubbing together can cause serious irritation, it is obvious that these should be avoided whenever possible. Benadryl and Chlortrimeton are two common brands of this kind of medication. Sleep aids such as Nytol and Sominex also contain antihistamines and manifest these same negative side effects. Combined with alcohol, sedative antihistamines and sleep aids can be extremely dangerous, even fatal.

Fortunately, many prescribed antihistamines are now more successful at alleviating allergic symptoms, and the side effects that might accompany their use are considerably gentler. Medications such as Claritin (loratadine) and Hismanal (astemizole) are generally considered nonsedating antihistamines. Their use in treating many allergic disorders is considered "state of the art" and should be used in preference to older sedating antihistamines that cause lethargy and drying of the mucous membranes.

Antacids such as Axid, Tagamet, Pepcid, and Zantac are commonly taken to ease the symptoms of "heartburn." Today there is more appreciation of problems created by gastroesophageal reflux on the larynx and throat. Varying degrees of reflux can cause acid taste, chronic cough, hoarseness due to irritation of the vocal folds, or pain in the chest. These conditions require medical consultation and can often be treated with lifestyle changes, such as eating smaller meals, elevating the head of the bed while sleeping, avoiding foods that might aggravate the situation, and reducing smoking and alcohol consumption.

Local anesthetics, found in some throat sprays and lozenges, can be particularly misleading. While offering the sore throat victim immediate comfort, they can lull the singer into a false sense of well-being, which can result in overuse of the voice and consequent vocal damage. Since singing is largely monitored by feel, local anesthetics can present problems of the most serious kind. A sore throat accompanied by redness and fever usually indicates infection and should be treated by a physician. Discomfort not accompanied by these symptoms often indicates mouth breathing or an allergy flare-up and can be reduced by drinking warm liquids.

Vitamin C, ascorbic acid, has been reported as beneficial in preventing viral infections. Like antihistamines, large quantities (over two grams) of vitamin C can be drying and induce diuresis (frequent urination) leading to dehydration. If taken over an extended period of time, its consumption may stimulate the production of kidney stones.

Social drugs, such as marijuana, cocaine, and alcohol, are infamous for the ways in which they disturb bodily function. On stage, as in life, the side effects can be deadly. Singing, like sports, demands absolute concentration with all faculties intact. Despite the frequently reported irresponsible antics of some in-the-news performers, users of social drugs, because of the chemical components they ingest, can count on performing far below their potential best. The use of *tranquilizers* such as Valium, Xanax, and Librium also diminishes physical and mental sensations which are needed to monitor and control vocal performance, and should be taken only when absolutely necessary.

Smoking, besides posing a general health risk, is a major irritant to the mouth, throat, and respiratory system. Fluid collects under the mucosa covering the vocal folds, and the mucosal surfaces become inflamed and damaged. Hoarseness and decreased range usually result. Smoking and singing are totally incompatible.

Halitosis, or bad breath, is a particularly difficult problem for singers. The causes of halitosis can include poor oral hygiene, dental or gum disease, oral lesions which allow the pocketing of food particles, and oral secretions. General measures to combat halitosis include a careful daily hygiene regimen with brushing and flossing and semi-annual dental examinations. Obviously, the consumption of odorous foods should be assiduously avoided.

Birth control pills which are predominantly estrogen appear to have little effect on most users. Pills which are primarily progesterone-based, however, can be another matter. Closely related to testosterone, progestins can have a masculinizing effect on the female larynx. Androgens are even worse in this respect. If this type of medication is used to treat menstrual problems or endometriosis, a laryngologist must be consulted before treatment is begun.

Chemotherapy, sometimes required to combat malignancy, may involve drugs of the most powerful kind for which there is no viable alternative. It can affect the vocal range of the female singer, but its potential benefit far outweighs the loss of a few high notes.

Blood pressure pills such as Inderal are sometimes prescribed to lessen stage fright. They can suppress the elevation of blood pressure and heart rate necessary to respond to the challenges of performance without addressing the causative factors. As with other drugs which encourage these problems, this type of medication should be avoided when possible in situations where the singer's health will not be negatively affected.

Diuretics, also used in the treatment of high blood pressure and certain premenstrual symptoms, promote the excretion of sodium and fluid. The obvious danger for singers is the possibility of less mucous secretion in the larynx, thereby increasing the probability of underlubricated vocal folds. The result can be the same as that described for other kinds of drying medication, voice fatigue, and hoarseness. In addition, they are ineffective in removing the type of swelling resulting in "veiled" premenstrual voice.

Pesticides, paint fumes from oil based paint, and other inhaled toxins are other sources of irritation to the voice. A high number of pesticides are thought to dissolve in body fat, never to be eliminated, and should be carefully avoided.

Surgical procedures are commonplace and a particular concern for performers. Regardless of the type of surgery, anesthesiologists should always be notified when the patient is a singer and asked to be especially cautious when introducing and removing endotracheal tubes. If a physician identifies *nodules, polyps,* or *cysts* (growths on the vocal folds), this diagnosis should be confirmed by a laryngologist experienced in evaluating and treating singers.

Strobovideolaryngoscopy can objectively measure vocal and pulmonary function. Speech and singing voice evaluation should also be performed before surgery is contemplated. Nodules, in particular, are often the result of misuse of the voice (talking or singing too loudly, too long, too high, or too much at the same pitch) and can be corrected with the help of a good voice teacher and speech pathologist.

Voice rest may be prescribed as part of the recuperation routine following an acute injury or surgery. Total rest, when written communication is needed, is rarely recommended for more than two weeks. Relative voice rest, speaking only when necessary, is generally helpful whenever the vocal folds are affected by fatigue, illness, or injury. It should also be noted that both whistling and whispering may exert significant strain on the vocal folds. Singers should refrain from these activities during the time when voice rest is required.

Exercise is no longer considered an option to healthy living. It is clearly a fundamental necessity as critical to staying physically fit as proper hygiene and nutrition. Without question, it has been shown to benefit the muscular, vascular, nervous, and respiratory systems and to promote a positive emotional attitude. The importance to good singing of a generally healthy body cannot be overlooked or underestimated. It takes attention and it takes work.

SEVEN

Theatrics of Singing

The ultimate goal of most singers is to share their music, either as a member of a group or as a soloist. The conductor or director of a group explains its style of presentation to performers, but solo singers must choose their own.

Most singers, when they first begin to perform, are extremely nervous. Frankly, in fact, it can be counted on. But as performances progress, there is an increase in the ease and effectiveness with which one sings. Singers, unlike instrumentalists, do not express themselves through an object apart from their person. They literally expose themselves to success and failure. Regardless of circumstances, committed singers keep working and sharing. Focusing intense concentration on giving to the audience often helps channel the increased energy felt in the preperformance hours, and "being," not "acting," the character adds captivating magnetism on stage.

To become a charismatic singing performer, which is, after all, the ultimate goal, it is highly advisable to study piano, acting, and movement (fencing, dance, and so on). The contribution of all of these to a high-quality performance in every style of singing, from pop to opera, is enormous. These disciplines need not be studied exhaustively—even two years' work in each would be helpful—but the importance of their integration into performance preparation cannot be overemphasized.

The study of piano is important because of the basic musical knowledge it can afford. It is essential for intelligent communication with accompanists, or with a conductor in a group situation. If students periodically hum along with music they are playing during their practice session, a facility in sight reading will often develop rapidly. In addition, much will be learned about basic musical terminology concerning volume levels and expression markings.

Studying acting is helpful in order to learn to project and to concentrate, to think thoughts appropriate to a given character or situation. To interpret a song honestly it is important to master the technique of having thoughts logically connected to the song, not only while conveying the text, but also during instrumental introductions, interludes, and conclusions. For example, during an instrumental introduction, singers should not contemplate the temperature of the room or the possible reactions to their performance. Instead, if one is singing "Beneath a Weeping Willow's Shade," the singer might picture a girl in eighteenth-century dress, sitting under a willow, despairing over the departure of her loved one. The dominant attitude the performer might adopt for this song—and one must always be adopted—might be compassion. This attitude, and visualization of the pictures and thoughts of the text, must be maintained, without interruption, until the conclusion of the song.

In addition, acting, which, like singing, is a learned technique, will introduce the singer to various ways of using the body to communicate ideas and feelings. This is another critical aspect of effective presentation of all styles. "Feeling it," without training in the specifics and effects of movement, is, like singing naturally, almost never good enough. Courses in acting fundamentals and programs integrating voice, acting, and dance, such as music theatre or opera workshops, are absolutely essential for a singer of any style of music.

Like acting, movement, and specifically dance, gives performers an awareness of the picture they are making onstage, and will teach them to project energetically to an audience. From ballet to jazz, much can be learned about posture and stance, and the impact caused by even the smallest gesture. Fencing is helpful for male singers, particularly in the area of operatic singing.

Broadly speaking, there are three general categories or styles of singing, as noted earlier. They are classical, popular, and theater. For the sake of versatility, a performer will sometimes cross over from one category to another. But the general practice is that one of the styles will usually be of considerably greater appeal to a singer than the other two, and in that one the performer will specialize. Songs in the anthology in this volume are taken from all three areas. Because the manner of presentation for every style varies considerably, a brief overview of each will be given.

Classical singing, which includes opera, oratorio, and recital, as well as most "legitimate" music for the church, demands, by tradition, that a great deal be communicated with practically no stage movement. As in the other areas, much can be communicated by stance. If the song is prayerful, it might well by sung with the feet placed more closely together. If the song is assertive, the feet might be planted firmly apart. The singer might lean slightly forward if the character of the song is telling a story, particularly with an excited or earnest attitude. One might lean somewhat backward if the song conveys a passive or depressed text. The singer seldom, if ever, takes a step during the song. In a recital setting, the singer might choose to stand close to the piano, in its curve, while singing something of an intimate nature, such as a lullaby, and somewhat in front of it for an assertive song, such as a sea chanty.

The visual focus in all styles of singing is determined by the text of the song. A narrative song, such as "Early One Morning" (see the anthology), will by sung looking directly at the audience (periodically changing the place of focus, in accordance with the music). "How Could I Ever Know?" because of the deeply personal nature of its text, should be sung directly to the imagined person being addressed, with minimal shift of focus and virtually no body movement.

Songs of the classical type, called *art songs*, are performed exactly as the composer wrote them. With the exception of contemporary music, there is usually no extemporaneous styling. Spontaneous expression, a vital part of all performances, must fit well within the dictates of the composer's score. Classical singers must also prepare songs and arias in several languages besides English—notably, Italian, French, German, and Spanish.

Since performances of classical music are usually not electronically amplified, the classical singer is trained to sing without benefit of a microphone, which is good discipline for theater and pop singers also.

Dress for the classical singer is usually formal. Suits or tuxedos for men are the norm, with long dresses for women. Solid-colored dresses with long sleeves will focus attention on the singer's face. Prints on a dress fabric are often distracting. Basic rules for good dressing apply to onstage performance as well. Numerous books are available on the subject.

Audiences frequently pass abiding judgment on a performer during the first minute onstage. Because of that, and because an entrance can be used to help set a mood for a program, it should be worked through carefully and practiced many times. When it is time to go onstage, the singer should locate a spot to stand where the lights will show him to best advantage. Then one should walk confidently to that predetermined spot, looking straight ahead. It is important never to look down, since a lowered gaze can signify confusion or discomfort to an audience. For a smooth walk, the abdominals should be contracted, as in dance, and the arms should move in opposition to the feet. As the singer greets the audience, during both entrances and bows, friendliness and an enormous desire to communicate must be projected. Finally, handing music to an accompanist, if that is necessary, should be carefully practiced, making sure that the singer's profile, not his posterior, is facing the room.

Popular singing currently includes many styles, such as folk, country, jazz, and rock. In pop singing, the emphasis is on individuality, both in dress and presentation. The performer in this style of music is encouraged to be "packaged" as uniquely as possible. Dress is determined, very often, by the type of picture the performer wishes to present to enhance the style of music being sung. Concert videos are filled with examples. Stage movements for the pop singer might run the gamut from that described for the classical singer to a no-holds-barred, carefully choreographed dance routine.

Good microphone technique is a must. "Paging" the mike, the moving of the cord back in the direction of the amplifier while holding the mike in the opposite hand, requires considerable practice. Also, experimentation is necessary to figure out the proper distance from the singer's mouth to the microphone in order to ensure the desired vocal effect. For more "presence," intensified contact, in an intimate song, the microphone must be held close to the singer. For high or loud tones, the distance will be greater.

To secure a club date, the pop singer needs to have thoroughly prepared in excess of forty songs of various types, which are divided into groups, or *sets*. Sets, each containing approximately six songs, can be assembled using different strategies. One basic pattern might resemble the following:

Opener	positive text, up-tempo
Credibility Song	sincere lyrics, slower than the opener
Slow Song	
Song of Choice	new or unfamiliar
False Ending	dramatic, up-tempo
Encore	more subdued than the False Ending, meaningful for the audience

Sets must be assembled with careful thought to the overall effect of the various styles, harmonies, and lyrics.

Pop songs are usually learned from *lead sheets* (see Figure 7.1), on which only the melody line is given and the letter names for chords indicated. That is, no specific notes are indicated for the accompaniment, so that instrumentalists are free to improvise. Unlike classical and theater singing, the performance of popular songs in transposed keys, either higher or lower than they were originally written, is not only acceptable, but expected. Original arrangements of a song, which often completely change its mood, are highly desirable, as long as the new arrangements relate well to the lyrics or the environment of the performance.

Since, at the moment, some commercial sounds that are selling best require men to sing in the head and falsetto registers and women to sing primarily in the chest and middle registers, pop singers will frequently sing higher or lower than they would if they were doing classical or theater singing. But because singers should vocalize over at least a three-octave range, this adjustment in ranges should be comfortable if all other aspects of good vocal production are heeded. If vocal difficulties arise from an attempt to sing a song,

FIGURE 7.1

Excerpt from lead sheet

the pitches of the melody can be modified to accommodate the performer.

Owing to its origins, the category of singing most influenced by the theater is musical theater. The ability to "project" dramatically frequently precedes most musical considerations, especially in the early training of new musical theater performers. "Belting," a style of singing done at a loud volume level in which the chest register is used to its uppermost limits, is taught as a quick way to add energy to a singing performance. Although it is absolutely necessary to belt in order to effectively portray many characters in a musical theater production, ultimately this technique is far from desirable in terms of vocal health. As with any style of extreme vocal production, it should be carefully monitored. On the other hand, the idea of portraying a rough-spoken character using only dialogue, and reverting to a refined style of singing for that person's songs, is totally incongruous. It is extremely important that theater students take great pains to develop an excellent singing technique, so that they can use voice production suitable to different types of characters. They need to be aware of the potential vocal hazards that might occur, and know how to create their roles in a vocally healthy manner. Hoarseness, often heard among actors, is not an indication of vocal health and can be avoided.

"Selling" the song, in all styles of singing, is the fundamental goal. Specifically, "selling" refers to dramatic components, including energy level, concentration, and characterization. For the successful musical theater performer, all these must be present to the greatest extent possible. Although stage and/or body microphones are almost always used for theater productions, enormous energy must emanate from the actors themselves.

For musical theater auditions, songs are sung only in the original keys and by performers for whom they are appropriate. (Some of the theater songs in the anthology have been transposed for convenience in class use.) For example, a man's song is never sung by a woman, using modified lyrics. A director will usually indicate whether songs are to be sung from the show being cast or from other shows. Failure to pay attention to the director's request indicates laziness and insufficient interest in the show and frequently eliminates a performer form consideration. Again, selling a "package" is of the utmost importance. The auditioner should always be familiar with the proposed show and try to look, sing, and act similar to, but not exactly like, the character one hopes to play. An attempt to identify totally with a character might well work to the auditioner's disadvantage, since the director often has strong ideas about characterizations and needs to feel an actor is willing to be flexible enough to create the role as the director sees fit. It is important to inquire about the director's preferences.

Because performers for musical theater auditions must often dance as well as read and sing, they must come dressed ready to move. They should be well-groomed, with the hair back from the face, and should look nicely dressed. Stylish jeans and a T-shirt or a leotard with a wraparound skirt, or other dance clothes, are often the most appropriate apparel.

As the discussion of the three categories of singing has proceeded, it has been seen that, although there are major differences among them, they have much in common. A sense of appreciation for performers in all styles is certainly in order. As singers first begin to perform, it cannot be expected that the proficiency they have attained during private practice will be retained in performance. To learn to concentrate and communicate in performance takes persistent effort. Gradually, however, singers will notice—with pleasure—that they are becoming more skilled and effective before an audience.

And pleasure, after all, is what music is all about.

EIGHT

Music Reading

It happens often that while searching for music, singers will find a song that they have heard only once or twice. They like the text as well as the music, but cannot remember exactly how the melody moves. Choir members sometimes have parts they wish they could learn prior to a rehearsal. A pianist is not always available, and for that reason, it is highly advisable to develop some ability to read music.

One of the fastest ways to learn this skill, which is really not difficult and only takes practice, is to enroll in a beginning piano or music reading class. As a brief introduction, here is a summary of some of the basic facts.

All traditional music is written on a five-line structure called a staff.

Commonly, higher pitches are indicated in the G clef, or *treble clef,*

while low pitches are shown in the F clef, or *bass clef.*

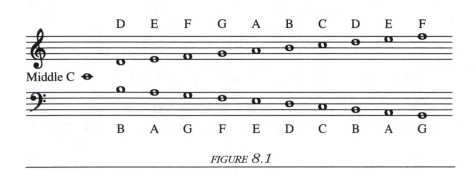

FIGURE *8.1*

The most frequently sung pitches are drawn on the staffs above (see Figure 8.1). Although both clefs extend beyond these points, the illustration begins at middle C, a note located near the insignia above the piano keyboard, at its center.

For years, many people have used mnemonic devices to memorize the letter names of the pitches quickly (for instance, *All Cows Eat Grass*) in which the first letter of each word is the same as a note on the staff (see Figure 8.2). In the case of *All Cows Eat Grass*, the letters correspond to the letter names of the notes located in the spaces (between the staff lines) of the bass clef. *Good Boys Do Fine Always* may be used to help memorize the notes on the lines. These sentences always work from the bottom to the top of the staff. The classic *Every Good Boy Does Fine* assists with learning the notes on the lines in the treble clef, and the letters of the word *FACE* are the same as the notes in the spaces of the treble clef.

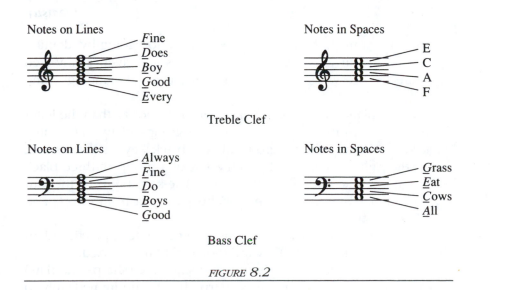

FIGURE *8.2*

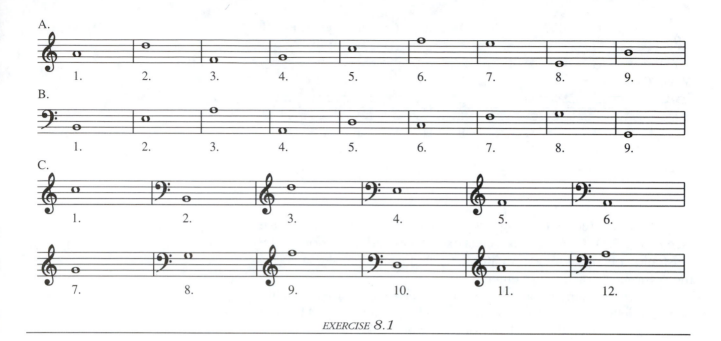

EXERCISE 8.1

EXERCISE 8.1

At this point, it might be helpful to review the foregoing by identifying the pitches in Exercise 8.1. (the answers are given in inverted type directly below it). For more review, use a beginning piano book.

On the piano keyboard, even easier to memorize than the letter names of notes, one can readily spot the groups of two and three black keys. To the left of a group of two black keys is always a C, and to the right of them, an E. To the left of a group of three black keys is an F, and to the right of them, a B. The keys between the four keys mentioned are arranged in alphabetical order from A to G and simply repeat that pattern.

Using the keyboard and covering its typed letters, practice identifying the white keys until they are thoroughly memorized.

At the beginning of a song, the key signature (sharps and flats) is usually indicated. A piano key's sharp (♯) is found immediately to its right, while its flat (♭) is found immediately to its left. A sharp will sound higher than the natural key, while the flat will sound lower.

Flats and sharps can be white keys or black keys. The pitches to which the key signature applies can be determined by figuring out the name of the pitch that is located in the same place as the sharp or flat. For example,

indicates a flat on the third line of the treble clef. The note always found on the third line of the treble clef is a B; therefore, the flat indicates a B-flat. This means that any B found in the music, even though it may be higher or lower, will be flatted.

Locate the flats and sharps of all the white keys.

The component of music reading that requires the most practice for many is rhythm. The staff is divided into *measures* by vertical lines. A *time signature*, at the beginning of a song, consists of two numbers, one above the other. The upper number indicates the number of beats per measure; the lower number shows the type of note that gets one beat. In the time signature $^4/_4$, the upper 4 shows that there are four beats per measure, while the lower 4 means that a quarter note gets one beat. In a $^3/_8$ time signature, there are three beats per measure, and an eighth note gets one beat.

Figure 8.3 lists the most common rhythmic values used in notation. When a dot follows a note, it becomes a half again as long as it would ordinarily be. For example, when a note that gets two beats is followed by a dot, it would then get three beats.

Practice clapping the rhythms in Exercise 8.2. When they can be clapped without hesitation, recite, or pencil in, the letter names of the pitches to which the rhythms correspond. When the letter names can be recited readily, recite and clap them in rhythm. Next, practice playing the melodies on the keyboard. (Melodies for songs may be approached in the same manner.)

Whole Note	𝅝		= 4 beats
Half Note	𝅗𝅥	or 𝅗𝅥	= 2 beats
Quarter Note	♩	or ♩	= 1 beat
Eighth Note	♪	or ♪	= ½ beat
Sixteenth Note	𝅘𝅥𝅯	or 𝅘𝅥𝅯	= ¼ beat

FIGURE 8.3

EXERCISE 8.2

Rests, or silences, are designated in a manner similar to that for notes (see Figure 8.4). For example, the whole rest usually gets four beats.

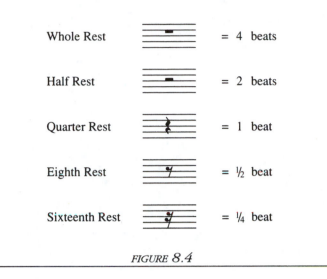

Whole Rest		= 4 beats
Half Rest		= 2 beats
Quarter Rest		= 1 beat
Eighth Rest		= ½ beat
Sixteenth Rest		= ¼ beat

FIGURE 8.4

Play the melody in Exercise 8.3. It should sound familiar.

EXERCISE 8.3

PART *II*

Song Anthology

Background and Performance Notes

Performance Notes

While preparing songs for performance, the following general guidelines should be implemented:

- Breaths should be taken at nondisruptive places in the text, usually at commas, periods, or rests.

- To sing a smooth, connected line, vowels should be sustained, and the final sound of each word should be attached to the first sound of the word which follows.

- Consonants—particularly initial ones—in the most colorful and significant words of a text should be especially emphasized.

- Indicated dynamics should be incorporated for expressive singing.

- Song texts should be mentally visualized, even during rests, to best convey the emotional meaning of a song.

Folk Songs

The origins of early folk songs are often unknown. These songs evolved musically and textually as they were passed along by oral tradition and have existed in many different versions. Many are hundreds of years old and have traditionally flourished in rural areas where opportunities for publication did not exist. Some songs are simple, others complex.

Today folk songs are set in many different musical styles. The song texts, often available in several versions, usually deal with events of everyday life. Songs about love, death, and hardship are common, as are lullabies, drinking songs, patriotic narratives, and dance tunes. More than any other style, folk songs reflect the concerns and mores of their time and place. These songs are the source for much of today's popular music.

Because each country's folk music often shares characteristic features, songs are listed in alphabetical order under their assumed country of origin.

America (United States)

Since America is a relatively new country with constantly changing patterns of immigration, it is impossible to describe a specific music of "the folk." Native Americans have enjoyed a thriving song culture, but partially due to complicated language barriers, this music has not been influential on the mainstream popular-folk tradition.

The strongest influence on early American folk music has traditionally been the music of European settlers from England, France, Germany, Ireland, and Italy. Since the late nineteenth century, songs using African music and rhythms have enjoyed widespread popularity, as has music from several Latin American countries. Currently the rising number of Asian residents promises to further enrich the American folk music scene.

Originally, the unwritten tradition of passing along melodies did not take hold as strongly in the industrialized northern states, where classical and theater music flourished. But in the more rural southern states, highly developed, even virtuostic musical styles such as jazz and bluegrass emerged from African slave songs, Southern Baptist hymnody, and dance music of the Appalachian Mountains. In the two decades following 1950, singers like Woody Guthrie, Bob Dylan, and Pete Seeger actively prompted a widespread enthusiasm for American folk music. Texts often highlighted the struggle for peace, freedom, and justice, as well as the burdens and joys of everyday life.

"Black Is the Color of My True Love's Hair" (page 80)   This romantic folk ballad originated about 1875 and reveals a lover's infatuation that grows in intensity through the first three verses and is reaffirmed in the fourth. "Black, black, black" should be sung with the most emphasis placed on the third "black" as it leads and is connected to the rest of the thought. No breath should be taken until the period following "hair."

"Troublesome" refers to a creek in Eastern Kentucky.

"The Juniper Tree" (page 98)   This song relates the happy memory of a time when a younger sister was handed a hat and teasingly sent off to find a man. "And one or two kisses will do you no harm, I know, I know," carries the implication that the singer has been there before and knows whereof he speaks. Juniper trees are evergreens and are found in many areas of North America.

The feel of the song should be buoyant and fun, with the first beat of each measure mildly accented.

"My Dearest Love, Why Wilt Thou Ask" (page 104)   One of the older entries in this anthology, this song was found in a collection of tavern songs sung in colonial Williamsburg, Virginia, around 1700. The notation indicates a dominantly long-short-long-short rhythmic pattern to which the melody is set. It is necessary to watch for exceptions to this pattern as the song is being learned.

This is a smooth, floating, yet fervent ballad originally sung with guitar accompaniment.

"Shady Grove" (page 125)   Many well-loved American folk songs have came from the people of the Appalachian Mountains, which extend from Quebec to northern Alabama. This contagious dance tune with its breezy melody and high-spirited rhythm is a popular standby with banjo and fiddle players and has been passed along for generations.

England

England's folk traditions are different from those of the other British Isles, in part because of the impact of the industrial revolution in the late eighteenth century. Many British folk songs were first heard during that time. But even as English culture became more urban and cosmopolitan, the rural lifestyles in Ireland, Scotland, and Wales remained much as they had been, nurturing the continuation of a strong folk music heritage.

Numerous English folk songs are melodic and sophisticated and appear to be closely related to "art" music of the time. Some of the styles include *carols* (seasonal songs composed since the fifteenth century), *shanties* (sailors' work songs), lullabies, and ceremonial and country dances. A significant part of this repertoire has been set to classical instrumental and vocal music forms that are still highly appealing to today's audiences.

"The Crystal Spring" (page 86) This traditional English song gives an account of one side of the conversation between a persuasive captain and his would-be bride. Unfamiliar words might be *proffer*, "suggest"; *chaffing*, "teasing"; and *wind*, which in this instance takes the Middle English pronunciation and rhymes with *kind*. Care should be taken to give clarity and meaning to this episode retold.

"Early One Morning" (page 91) This is the recounting of a soliloquy overheard. The song is empathetic, tinged with anguish. In order, the verses are forthright, urgent, hopeful, and chagrined, with the most heartfelt plea saved for the end. This song is full of *arpeggios* which generally utilize every other note in a musical scale. Continuous contraction of the abdominal muscles and evenly exhaled breaths throughout the singing of each phrase will contribute to a uniform tone quality throughout the range of this melody.

"The Trees They Do Grow High" (page 129) This familiar folk song is unique to this anthology because of the three perspectives found in the text. The story is told first by the maid, then by her father, and finally by the narrator. It relates the tale of an arranged marriage between the girl and a handsome but immature boy (some versions of the song put his age at fourteen) who becomes what her father predicts, but perishes in his prime.

Changes in the characters describing this tragic account will necessitate changes in dramatic attitude and, therefore, vocal presentation. Unfamiliar words might include *bide*, "to live together"; and *bonny lad*, "good-looking boy."

"True Lover's Farewell" (page 134)   A conversational episode is retold in this dialogue between a departing lover and his uncertain lady. His promises of loyalty are met with grieving and doubt, punctuated by the reference to the lamenting dove. Again it should be noted that changes in characterization require adjustment in the style of presentation, in this instance on alternating verses.

Ireland

The folk music tradition in Ireland enjoys a thriving tradition to this day. As in England, the majority of commonly sung songs actually originated in the eighteenth and nineteenth centuries. Irish folk instruments include fiddles, whistles, drums, bagpipes, and harps.

Love songs are the most common lyrical pieces; the best are highly expressive, with rich poetic images. There are also silly songs meant simply for fun, and countless dance songs—triple-time *jigs*, fast duple-time *reels,* and slower duple-time *hornpipes.*

"The Kerry Dance" (page 101)   One of Ireland's best-known tunes, this song, with its infectious melody, recalls bucolic evenings in the glens (valleys) of county Kerry. The euphoric effect of the nights and the music are remembered by one whose youth has, regrettably, passed.

Reflecting its dance origin, heavily accented downbeats begin every measure, and ornamental notation, serving as a dramatic stress, is found over the word *wild.*

"Oh, to think of it, oh, to dream of it, fills my heart with tears!" is a happy exclamation preceding the final refrain.

Italy

The folk and art music traditions of Italy are long and varied, exhibiting pronounced regional distinctions. Some of the music of northern Italy is surprisingly similar to that of the Anglo-Scottish tradition. Instruments of the herdsmen in that Alpine region include fiddles, accordions, and even bagpipes.

The southern and Mediterranean regions of the country typically enjoy lyrical melodies influenced by Greek and North African cultures, while the folk music of central Italy tends to be florid and virtuostic, featuring improvisational contests between solo singers.

Many of Italy's most famous folk songs are so profoundly influenced by operatic repertoire, popular since the seventeenth century, that they can almost be considered on par with art songs of other countries.

"Santa Lucia" (page 122)   This heavily sentimental favorite paints a shimmering picture of a balmy night as local residents row out to greet the ship *Santa Lucia*. Excited calls from the sailors can be heard as they approach the shores of their beloved Naples.

The first note in each group of two eighth-notes over the words "Santa Lucia" should be lightly accented. An even vibrato, always a measure of good breathing, should be maintained throughout the arpeggios in the refrain.

Jamaica

The native inhabitants of Jamaica were killed during the age of the Spanish exploration. From then on, the island was populated by European colonists and their African slaves. As slavery persisted, Africans dominated the population: The texts of Jamaican folk songs are usually *creole*, a blend of English, French, Spanish, and various African languages.

Jamaican music is primarily influenced by the African musical tradition. Several types of folk songs exist: ritualistic, informative, ceremonial, work, and leisure songs. Favorite instruments include drums, conventional and adapted guitars, wooden banjos, flutes, and violins. Calypso music originated in Trinidad and Tobago and is intended as popular entertainment.

"Always One Rain" (page 75) Perhaps one of the most catchy melodies among the folk songs in this anthology, this lively tune takes a good-natured look at a hard-to-cope-with subject. Like the texts of many calypso songs, this relies heavily on the vernacular.

The presence of *syncopation,* the musical practice of stressing weak beats or weak parts of beats, is the most obvious departure from the rest of the folk songs included in this volume. Obvious in such parts of the text as "bright *sun*-light" and "lit-*tle* cloud," syncopation is also used frequently in the song refrain. It is often indicated by dotted notes, eighth notes, or both. Syncopation gives calypso music strong appeal, but requires extra concentration in the learning process to ensure that all rhythms are sung with accuracy.

The concept behind the song title can be taken literally, since rainfall in some of the mountainous parts of Jamaica can in fact exceed 200 inches per year—five times the world average.

Peru

The diverse people of Peru are divided among the simple tribes of the rain forest, the descendants of the Incas, and a mixed group which represents general Andean culture. European musical styles, introduced by Spanish explorers, combined with instruments indigenous to the three population groups—notably wood whistles, gourds, flutes, and pan-pipes—combine to give Peruvian music its unique sound.

"The River" (El Rio) (page 118)   This strophic song extols contentment as the sum of life's parts in the symbolism of the flowing river. As the river blends the experiences of those who touch it, so too does the human journey. Colorful and significant words in the text should be emphasized, and, as always in songs of multiple verses, special attention needs to be given to telling the story.

Scotland

Two distinct regions divide the country of Scotland: the sparsely populated, mountainous Highlands and the narrow Lowlands where the majority of the population resides. Both regions are famous for the use of bagpipes in their regional music, as well as fiddles and harps.

For centuries, Scottish ballads have told of legendary characters like King Arthur. Favorite work songs, originally functional, helped coordinate physical tasks like spinning and rowing and made the time pass more quickly. Frequently nonsense syllables like *hi-ree-hi-ra-lee* and *hey-nonny-nonny* are included for the sake of maintaining rhythm.

As in England, some Scottish folk songs were collected and published about 1600, but in the eighteenth century, an eruption of political, social, and religious ideas inspired a wealth of material that was set to song. Although the spoken language is English, a small percentage of the population speaks a Gaelic-based dialect that can sometimes be found in the music of this country.

"Flow Gently, Sweet Afton" (page 95)   This simple lyrical song is arguably among the most famous folk songs of all time. The accompaniment reflects the gentleness of the flowing river and the tenderness of the moment. Several words in the text might be unfamiliar, including: *braes,* "hillsides"; *stock dove,* "pigeon"; *yon',* "distant"; *dell,* "small valley"; *lapwing,* "bird with a shrill cry"; *forbear,* "cease"; *cot,* "cottage"; *wanton,* "unrestrained"; *lave,* "wash"—rhymes with *wave*; and *lays,* "songs." The *fermata* (⌢) over the second *Afton* indicates a held note and is also applicable to *flowrets* in the second verse.

"My Love Is like a Red, Red Rose" (page 107)   This beloved song lyrically declares undying love even though distance should cause temporary separation. The range of the melody is wider than many other folk songs and adds to the dramatic intensity. The *triplet,* requiring the singing of three notes on one beat over the words *Oh my,* is frequently heard in the Scottish folk music tradition as well as in the music of many other countries, and should be given the same excellent voice quality required for the rest of the melody.

South Africa

South African folk tradition is widely diverse, coming from various tribal and European sources. The music of the Bushmen, generally sung by female groups accompanying male dancers, is predominantly vocal, with complex rhythmic clapping and drums. The racially mixed Hottentots, with their distinctive clicking language, have historically enjoyed elaborate flute ensembles and drums.

Afrikaans music is closely related to the melodies of England and the United States. Many tunes were quite literally borrowed and given Afrikaans texts. Songs are usually short, written in major keys, and syllabic; the standard dance band consists of concertina, guitar, and violin augmented by other instruments.

"On the Top of the Hill" (page 115) This simple Afrikaner tune is offered in good-natured jest and reflects the Dutch heritage of that varied culture. With an accented two-beat feel, this song can be used to accompany the traditional *Boeremusiek* often danced at South African festivals. Dotted rhythms should be observed, and the octave interval concluding each verse sung with accurate intonation and consistent tone quality.

Songs from Musical Theater

Although a rich tradition of theater music has existed throughout history, the modern Broadway show as we know it evolved from the English, French, and German theatrical productions whose touring companies traveled around the United States in the late nineteenth and early twentieth centuries. During the first quarter of the twentieth century, Victor Herbert, originally a cellist in the pit orchestra at the Metropolitan Opera, wrote forty *operettas* (light operas), devising a musical style that appealed to lovers of popular and classical music alike. Meanwhile his contemporary George M. Cohan wrote and directed 40 plays, acted in or produced 150 others, and published 500 songs, including "Give My Regards to Broadway" and "You're a Grand Old Flag." During the Roaring Twenties, composers and lyricists like Sigmund Romberg (*The Student Prince*) and Jerome Kern (*Show Boat*) mounted major successes on New York stages. George and Ira Gershwin also wrote several successful shows featuring such classic theater songs as "I Got Rhythm," frequently combining the musical sophistication of classical composition with an affinity for African American music.

During the 1930s depressed economic conditions and the growing popularity of sound films created a general scarcity of good musicals on New York stages as many of the creative giants focused on Hollywood. One production, however, stood out. Gershwin's folk opera *Porgy and Bess*, though initially a financial disaster, emerged as a theatrical masterpiece.

In the 1940s composer Richard Rodgers and librettist Oscar Hammerstein II reinvogorated the Broadway scene with a succession of five shows. These musicals, *Oklahoma!*, *Carousel*, *South Pacific*, *The King and I*, and *The Sound of Music*, along with comedies, period pieces, and contemporary-feeling productions from such other composers as Alan Jay Lerner, Frederick Loewe, Frank Loesser, and Leonard Bernstein, were extremely popular over the next twenty-five years. Many songs introduced in shows like *Brigadoon*, *Guys and Dolls*, *My Fair Lady*, *West Side Story*, *Camelot*, *Fiddler on the Roof*, and *Hello, Dolly!* have become standards, performed by singers and instrumentalists alike.

Since 1965 musicals have continued to flourish, and many productions today are more elaborate and technically advanced than any that have preceded them. John Kander and Fred Ebb (*Cabaret*), Jerry Herman (*La Cage aux Folles*), Marvin Hamlisch (*A Chorus Line*), Stephen Sondheim (*A Little Night Music*), and Andrew Lloyd Webber (*Phantom of the Opera*) are among those who have made significant contributions to the grand tradition of the Broadway musical.

Film music, of course, has a different history and is primarily a post–World War I development. Contrary to popular belief, movies were never silent. Besides the obvious dramatic benefits of coupling sight and sound, live music was always played to help cover the din of primitive projection machines.

Initially, random musical choices, from French café music to classical favorites, were performed on whatever instruments were available, culminating in the "Mighty Wurlitzer" theater organ. In 1908 the first score specifically written to accompany a film was composed in France by classical composer Camille Saint-Saëns. Warner Brothers commercialized the sound process in the 1920s, and in 1930 *Sunny Side Up*, the first all-talking, singing, dancing movie musical, was written for the screen. During the thirties several stars of this genre were born—Maurice Chevalier, Jeanette MacDonald, and Ruby Keeler among them. Directors like Busby Berkeley, who staged entertainment extravaganzas, ensured a lasting place for the movie musical in Hollywood.

In the two decades that followed, film music became increasingly influenced by the popular music of the day, reflecting the transition from big band to rock. Songs became simpler and more melodic. During the late fifties and sixties, the work of such composers as Henry Mancini, Michel Legrand, and Dimitri Tiomkin, who wrote songs to enhance the story lines of specific films, brought a new level of musical excellence to movie scoring. Later movies would frequently incorporate independently written songs into the musical score, spurring record sales into the millions.

In 1977 the *Star Wars* double album with music by composer-conductor John Williams broke all sales records; orchestral music was back. About the same time, the soundtrack of *Saturday Night Fever* sold 20 million copies, inaugurating the commercial-rock trend in film scores. Both styles, classical and commercial, have gained widespread popularity in movies of the last two decades.

"Before I Gaze at You Again" (page 141)   Lerner and Loewe teamed for several projects prior to *Camelot,* including *Brigadoon, My Fair Lady, Paint Your Wagon,* and the movie musical *Gigi.* Frederick Loewe, the composer, and Alan Jay Lerner, the lyricist, derived the show from the Arthurian legends featuring plenty of medieval sport and splendor. Some critics feel that the remarkable success of this musical was due in part to its linkage to and the public's fascination with President John F. Kennedy.

The text relates a lover's heartbreak, the need for healing, and the admonition to "stay away until you cross my mind barely once a day"—in this moment of sorrow, a seemingly unlikely occurrence.

"Comes Once in a Lifetime" (page 146)   Jule Styne, a child prodigy on piano, collaborated with Stephen Sondheim (profiled under "No One Is Alone") on the show *Gypsy,* and scored numerous film and Broadway productions, including *Gentlemen Prefer Blondes* and *Funny Girl.* The plot of *Subways Are for Sleeping* depicts two unsteady love affairs in contemporary Manhattan, and in this particular song the attitude is one of seize-the-day enthusiasm. "Here's the rundown," sets the sportive tone culminating in "Only once comes this particular sky, Only once these precious hours will fly. Only once in a lifetime today comes by." The demeanor is philosophical, upbeat, and oh-so-tongue-in-cheek.

"How Could I Ever Know?" (page 150)   One of the most recently written entries in the anthology, this magnificent song is by contemporary composer Lucy Simon, sister of popular musician Carly Simon. From the show *The Secret Garden,* which tells the story of a lonely boy and his orphaned cousin, the song offers an often unspoken but profoundly felt message in the hearts of those who must be separated from ones they love through irreversible circumstances in life or death.

"Love Is a Many-Splendored Thing" (page 158)   Composer Sammy Fain, a veteran of movies and musicals, also produced successful popular songs for nearly fifty years, including "I'll Be Seeing You" and "Secret Love." This song, from the film of the same name, won the Academy Award in 1955. The film script is based on the true story of a female physician who falls in love with a war correspondent in Hong Kong during the Korean War. The melody is uncommonly beautiful and arguably among the classics of twentieth-century film music. The perspective is euphoric, the panorama wide.

"Love Walked In" (page 161)   George Gershwin is one of America's most important composers of concert, stage, and popular music. His works include jazz-influenced concert pieces like *Rhapsody in Blue* and the immortal folk opera *Porgy and Bess.* His first song "Swanee," written when he was nineteen, sold a million copies of sheet music and 2.5 million records.

His brother Ira was lyricist for much of Gershwin's music, this song included, which was sung several times in the film *The Goldwyn Follies.* The speech-like four-line introduction is used to set the scene for the more melodic refrain. In contrast to the comparatively free rhythm and styling of the first section, the second should be metrical and connected.

"Moon River" (page 168) Henry Mancini, prolific composer-arranger for film and television, recorded 85 albums and scored 250 movies, including *The Glenn Miller Story* and *The Pink Panther.* The commercial success of this song, from the film *Breakfast at Tiffany's,* strengthened the argument that every movie needs a hit tune. Its lyrics emphasize the idea that beneath a veneer of urban sophistication often lies a yearning for the simplicity of country life.

The flowing melodic line requires even, consistent breathing and vibrato to produce a tone quality that will effectively portray this scene of simple fantasy.

"No One Is Alone" (page 171) Stephen Sondheim was a protégé of Oscar Hammerstein II, a close family friend. At the age of twenty-five, Sondheim wrote the lyrics for Leonard Bernstein's *West Side Story,* and as composer-lyricist he has written a string of well-received, award-winning shows, including *A Funny Thing Happened on the Way to the Forum, A Little Night Music* ("Send In the Clowns"), *Sweeney Todd,* and *Sunday in the Park with George.*

Into the Woods is a show based on five of Grimm's fairy tales. This is a song of reassurance and was originally composed for an ensemble of characters.

"Once upon a Time" (page 176) College life and football set the scene for *All American,* the little-known production from which this song is taken. Composer Strouse and lyricist Adams had greater success prior to this show with *Bye Bye Birdie* and later with the ever popular *Annie.*

This uncomplicated song is a sad commentary on love gone awry. The wish that a second chance might be possible is hopelessly rejected in the closing phrase.

"The Shadow of Your Smile" (page 180) The "shadow" of a smile is a generally overlooked, yet inspired lyric. The sense of something lingering, yet unseen, is a haunting image, bringing peace or pain. This Academy Award–winning song by film composer Johnny Mandel was based on the theme for *The Sandpiper* and includes several wide intervallic leaps in its melody. Consistent breath support and voice quality are necessary to present this music expressively.

"Sometimes a Day Goes By" (page 186)   The Broadway musical *Woman of the Year,* based on the movie of the same name, is the story of a driven television personality and her nemesis/husband, a satirical cartoonist, who creates a comic strip character in her likeness. Composer John Kander and lyricist Fred Ebb have collaborated on numerous projects, including the shows *Cabaret* and *Chicago* and have, independently, created music and/or lyrics for television and film.

The futile effort and inevitable failure of trying to forget someone deeply loved is reflected in the text of this haunting song.

"Somewhere" (page 190)   *West Side Story* is a famous reworking of the Romeo and Juliet romance, with two rival teenage gangs substituting for the Montagues and Capulets. The song tells of two lovers' dream to escape the violence of New York City for a peaceful place where they can be together.

Leonard Bernstein was a highly successful and multifaceted composer of popular, concert, film, and Broadway works; he was also an internationally esteemed conductor, pianist, and television commentator. Lyricist Stephen Sondheim is profiled under "No One Is Alone."

"They Were You" (page 198)   *The Fantasticks,* the small production from which this song is excerpted, has been playing for more than thirty-five years in the tiny Off-Broadway theater where it premiered. The story concerns the parents of two adolescents who build a wall between their homes, thinking that the best way to keep their son and daughter together is to appear to keep them apart.

This simple waltz describes the happy outcome of the parents' efforts. The first beat of each measure should be lightly accented and a lyrical vocal quality maintained throughout the intervals of the melody.

"What Are You Doing the Rest of Your Life?" (page 202)   French composer Michel Legrand's career covers virtually every category of music: radio, television, jazz, popular, concert, and film music, including scores for *The Umbrellas of Cherbourg, The Thomas Crown Affair,* and *Yentl.* Alan and Marilyn Bergman meanwhile have contributed some of the most memorable song lyrics in twentieth-century popular and film music ("Little Boy Lost" and "The Way We Were"). Together, this team has created several masterpieces, this song among them.

Intimate and taken at a relaxed pace, the lyrics ask the ultimate question. The singer's emotions are heartfelt, centered around the hope that the life of the loved one will "begin and end with me."

"When You're Alone" (page 211)   John Williams is currently a leading orchestral conductor and composer of film music whose credits include: *Jurassic Park, Star Wars* and their sequels, and *Schindler's List*. Composer-lyricist Leslie Bricusse has written for a variety of films and shows including *Stop the World—I Want to Get Off, Victor/Victoria,* and *Home Alone.*

This song is taken from *Hook,* a film which updates the Peter Pan fairy tale. The childlike directness of this night song evokes the peace of a lullaby, trading the insecurity of nightfall for the serenity of heaven's light.

"Where or When" (page 215)   *Babes in Arms* is a show-within-a-show, as the children of vaudevillians present a revue to raise funds to keep themselves off a work farm. "Where or When?" stands out as the opening song. The introduction is introspective, full of speculation, and the lyrics build in confidence throughout the refrain. Rodgers and Hart collaborated on thirty shows during their long partnership. Hart's lyrics were among the first to express love in the second, rather than the third person (I love *you*), adding new intimacy to the meaning of popular and show ballads. Rodgers went on to team with Oscar Hammerstein II on such shows as *Oklahoma!, The King and I,* and *The Sound of Music.*

Art Songs and Arias

The development of the *art song* (also called concert song) can be traced to the fifteenth century, when secular music became more prominent and keenly differentiated from the sacred music of the church. Poetry almost always predated the music. The invention of the printing press at that time was an added stimulus, offering trained composers a means of publishing their music for distribution throughout Europe. Until about 1600, art songs were performed by ensembles, usually four voices, rather than by a soloist as they are today.

Along with folk songs, *opera,* first performed in Italy at the beginning of the seventeenth century, exerted a profound influence on the evolution of the art song. Opera presented all-sung dramatic stories and contained instrumental music, chorus, *recitative* (a type of speech-song used to move the dramatic action along), and the solo *aria.* Arias, the melodic, often reflective song-like sections of an opera, were eventually excerpted and sung independently of the operatic source, creating new performance standards and literature for trained singers. Henry Purcell is generally credited with adapting this form for English-speaking audiences in the late seventeenth century with his opera *Dido and Aeneas,* but other composers, particularly William Byrd and John Dowland, had previously written numerous songs which are frequently performed even in present-day recitals.

The music of different countries, though sharing many similarities, exhibited distinct characteristics. German art song, or *lied* (plural: lieder), flourished in the mid-eighteenth century following the era of Johann Sebastian Bach, George Frideric Handel (*Messiah*), Franz Joseph Haydn, and Wolfgang Amadeus Mozart, whose exquisite songs and arias were frequently part of larger choral and dramatic works. In the early nineteenth century, such lieder composers as Ludwig van Beethoven, Robert Schumann, and Franz Schubert began to "dress up" favorite folk songs that had enjoyed long-standing popularity, thereby creating new songs with accompaniments which more artistically reflected and embellished the poetic texts.

In the United States, professional composers established themselves around the mid-nineteenth century, when it was customary for most aspiring composers to spend a few years of study in Germany. Edward MacDowell (1860–1908) became the first American classical music composer of international renown.

Charles Griffes (1884–1920), Charles Ives (1874–1954), Aaron Copland (1900–1990), and Samuel Barber (1910–1981) are just a few of the composers who helped propel the American art song tradition to its fertile present. Today's composers—in the United States and many other countries—display a rich diversity of songwriting styles, some influenced by European music of the late nineteenth century, others pursuing highly individualized approaches to songwriting. Some composers continue to utilize native folk sources while their counterparts concentrate on harmonic and electronic possibilities.

"American Lullaby" (page 221)   Gladys Rich was an educator and active composer of sacred music, operetta, and songs. A product of the 1930s, this lullaby alludes to stocks, bridge (a card game), and the radio—three popular interests of the day. The accompaniment features a gentle rocking motion, while the melody is predictably simple and subdued. Since high notes are perceived as louder, the *mf* sections of the song should be performed with some restraint so as better to lull the restless child to sleep.

"Beneath a Weeping Willow's Shade" (page 225)   Musician, statesman, poet, essayist, inventor, church organist, and signer of the Declaration of Independence, Francis Hopkinson claimed to be the first "native-born American" (of European descent) to compose a song, "My days have been so wondrous free," in 1759. His music was influenced by aristocratic tastes of the day, notably a preference for Italian opera and the works of George Frideric Handel.

Words with unclear meanings might be: *plaintive,* "grief-stricken"; *lay,* a medieval song usually addressed to the Virgin Mary; *dulcet,* "sweet"; *Echo,* a nymph who pined away for love of the self-absorbed Narcissus; and *adieu,* "farewell."

"Bright Is the Ring of Words" (page 227)   Ralph Vaughan Williams was a famous twentieth-century English composer who composed symphonies, sacred and secular vocal music, instrumental pieces, and music for films and theater. He is well known for incorporating popular melodies into concert works.

Robert Louis Stevenson was a Scottish poet whose wide-ranging travels resulted in such divergent writing as *A Child's Garden of Verses* and *The Strange Case of Dr. Jekyll and Mr. Hyde*.

Contrasting dynamics play an important part in the performance of this contemplative song. The message: Good songs can touch the hearts of many generations.

"Early in the Morning" (page 234)   Ned Rorem is a preeminent composer of art songs. An American whose music holds broad international appeal, he lived nearly a decade in France and Morocco. This most timely of songs describes a scenario current even by today's standards and puts to rest the notion that art songs are irrelevant remnants of cultures long extinct.

The text describes a summertime "coffee break" at a Parisian outdoor café. It is located on the street Rue François Premier. The song setting reflects the idealistic outlook of a lovestruck twenty-year-old and finally hints at the reality life often teaches in matters of the heart.

Correct French pronunciation should be applied to the name of the street as well as to the menu items *croissants* and *café au lait*. The phrase "I was twenty and a lover, And in Paradise to stay" should be slightly relaxed, with the original tempo resumed on the final words of the text.

"If music be the food of love" (page 237)   Henry Purcell is one of the most important composers of the late seventeenth century and the father of English opera. He composed more than 200 songs, many of which are parts of larger works. This song survives in several versions and was intended for home performance with harpsichord accompaniment.

Words used commonly during Purcell's lifetime are *cloy*, "tiresome"; *mien*, "demeanor"; *transports*, "emotions"; and *feasted*, "sumptuously satisfied."

"Lachen und Weinen" (page 243)   Although he lived only thirty-one years, Franz Schubert composed more than 600 songs, as well as many other works. His songs are known for their lyrical nature and the exact fit of melody and accompaniment to poetic text.

This lied about the highs and lows of love describes the many moods of the heart. The meaning of every word in this and all foreign-language texts should be memorized to convey the content of the poem effectively.

"Liebst du um Schönheit" (page 251)   Clara Wieck was a virtuoso pianist, who in 1840 married her teacher, the famous composer Robert Schumann. Since it was at that time considered improper for a woman to be a composer, Clara's creative output was limited after her marriage. Performing, however, was considered acceptable, and she exerted a great influence on the musical taste of the time. She often played her husband's compositions as well as those of Johannes Brahms, a close friend. This song, one of about twenty she composed, extols the virtue of love in its highest form and discounts the passing nature of anything less.

"Long Have I Been with Grief Opprest" (page 259)   Despite its unknown origin, this song was published in 1730 in a ballad opera variously titled *The Female Parson* or *The Beau in the Suds*. Although it is not possible to establish this piece definitively as an art song in the formal context of that genre, it is, like other songs from larger works performed at this time, clearly representative of art song in the popular idiom.

A song of optimism, the poem communicates the triumph of good over pain and remembers that even in the midst of shadows, the sun is never far away. Music of this type was usually performed with harpsichord or guitar accompaniment.

"Loveliest of Trees" (page 263)   John Duke was an American pianist and composer who is primarily remembered for his many songs. Uncluttered and melodic, these melodies frame poetry, by A. E. Housman, of a similar kind.

The delicate white beauty of cherry blossoms at Eastertide is noted, as is the passage of time. The character in the poem remarks that at age seventy ("three score and ten"), he does not expect to see twenty more years, and that even fifty springs would not be enough to enjoy the magnificence of the season.

Adjustments in tempi and dynamics add dramatic impact to this song.

"O cessate di piagarmi" (page 268)   One of the foremost composers of the Italian *cantata* in the late seventeenth century, Scarlatti created more than 600 works of this genre. Consisting of two contrasting arias, each introduced by a recitative and sung by solo voice with instrumental accompaniment, these small narrative pieces were meant to be performed at home.

This aria is quiet, but intense, with a final entreaty at its conclusion. Because of the repetition, dramatic expression and contrasting dynamics are particularly important.

"Qué Pronto" (page 270)   Manuel Ponce, a well-respected Mexican composer, possessed a great gift for melody and is credited with bringing modern musical style to Mexican classical music. His song "Estrellita" became the most popular art song from that country and is performed internationally.

A simple but impassioned song about the universal misery of rejection, this song is tinged with anger, sarcasm, and anguish, the proportion of each to be decided by the performer. It is a realistic emotional mix, with numerous opportunities for nuance within relatively few lines.

"Se nel ben sempre incostante" (page 278)   Alessandro Stradella was a noted opera composer who, structurally and dramatically, heightened the style of the Italian aria. He was also one of the earliest composers to use the gradual volume increase indicated by the musical term *crescendo.*

This particular aria was taken from the opera *Le gare dell'amor eroico* (*The Contests of Heroic Love),* which was first performed in Genoa. The poetic text, or *libretto,* is a philosophical acknowledgment that, as Fortune sometimes changes in the midst of good times, so can it also change in the midst of bad.

"Think on Me" (page 284)   Alicia Ann Scott (Lady John Scott), whose name is indicative of her heritage, penned several well-received songs, the most recognized being "Annie Laurie." This song, published posthumously, seems to anticipate her death and offers love and encouragement to those left behind.

"When I was one-and-twenty" (page 288)   C. Armstrong Gibbs was an English composer who taught at the Royal College of Music in London. He wrote instrumental works, including symphonies, operas, and more than 100 songs.

The A. E. Housman poem comprising this text describes the regret ("rue") and sadness surrounding love given away too young and the frequently shortsighted wisdom of inexperienced hearts.

"Young Venevil" (page 294)   Frederick Delius was an English composer who "found himself" while growing oranges in Florida. Always an adventurer, he considered meeting Norwegian composer Edward Grieg to be one of the great events of his life, and Grieg's musical style greatly influenced Delius's music. In his later years, illness left Delius paralyzed and blind, but he continued to dictate music, including complete orchestral scores.

This narrative about the ardor and rejection of Venevil is told at a lively pace. Clarity of diction and dramatic and musical expression determine the exact tempo, the same criteria used for all styles of vocal performance.

Folk Songs

Always One Rain

Jamaica
Arranged by
Jean Shackleton

Background and Performance Notes, page 61

Calypso - Easily

Rain a day, __ To wash my tears a - way, __ There's

Al - ways One Rain, Al - ways One Rain,

Al - ways One Rain a day. _____

Words by
John Jacob Niles

Black Is the Color of My True Love's Hair

(High Voice)

United States
Arranged by
Jean Shackleton

Background and Performance Notes, page 58

With great tenderness

Black, black, black   is the col-or of my

true love's hair.   Her lips _____ are some-thing ro-sy fair.   The _ pert - est _ face and the
(His)   (pur - est _)

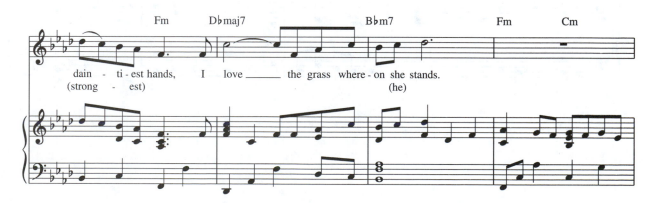

dain - ti - est hands,   I   love _____ the grass where - on she stands.
(strong - est)   (he)

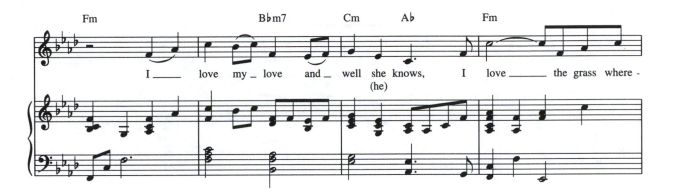

I ___ love my ___ love and ___ well she knows, I love ___ the grass where -
(he)

on she goes; If ___ she on ___ earth no ___ more ___ I ___ see, My life ___ will quick - ly
(he)   (he)

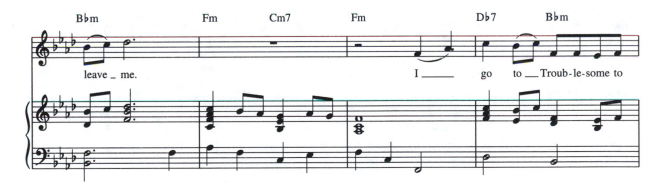

leave ___ me.   I ___ go to ___ Troub - le-some to

mourn, to weep, But sat - is-fied I ne'er can sleep; I'll ___ write her a note in a
(him)

81

few __ lit - tle lines, I'll suf - fer death ten thou - sand times.

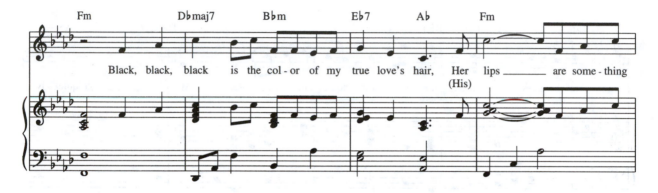

Black, black, black is the col - or of my true love's hair, Her lips _____ are some - thing
(His)

ro - sy fair, The __ pert - est __ face and the dain - ti - est hands, I
(pur - est _)   (strong - est)

love _____ the grass where - on she stands.
(he)

82

Words by
John Jacob Niles

Black Is the Color of My True Love's Hair

(Low Voice)

United States
Arranged by
Jean Shackleton

Background and Performance Notes, page 58

With great tenderness

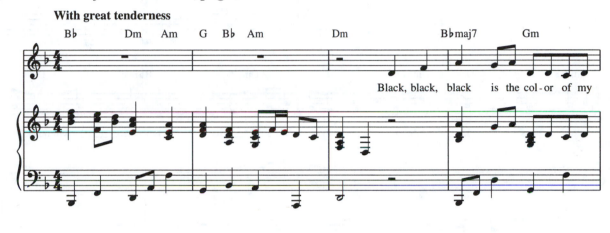

Black, black, black   is the col-or of my

true love's hair.   Her lips _____ are some-thing ro - sy fair.   The _ pert - est _ face and the
(His)   (pur - est _)

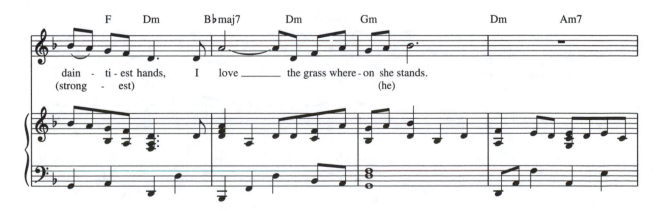

dain - ti - est hands,   I love _____ the grass where - on she stands.
(strong - est)   (he)

I ____ love my _ love and _ well she knows,   I ____ love _____ the grass where- (he)

on she goes;   If ____ she on _ earth no _ more _ I ____ see,   My life _____ will quick-ly (he)   (he)

leave _ me.   I _____ go to ____ Troub-le-some to

mourn, to weep,   But sat - is-fied I ne'er can sleep;   I'll __ write her a note in a (him)

few _ lit - tle lines, I'll suf - fer death ten thou-sand times.

Black, black, black is the col - or of my true love's hair, Her lips _____ are some - thing
(His)

ro - sy fair, The __ pert - est __ face and the dain - ti - est hands, I
(pur - est) (strong - est)

love _____ the grass where - on she stands.
(he)

The Crystal Spring

England
Arranged by
Jean Shackleton

Background and Performance Notes, page 59

cap - tain I spied, ___ En - treat - ing ___ his ___ true love for to

be ___ his bride.   2. O dear one ___ says ___

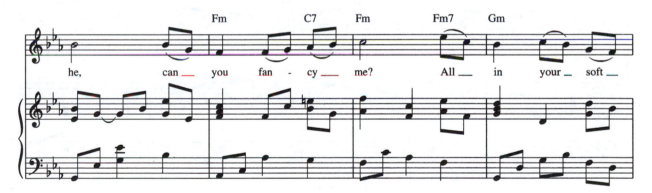

he,   can ___ you fan - cy ___ me?   All ___ in your ___ soft ___

bow - ers a crown it shall ___ be: You shall take ___ no

pain,   I ____ will you sus - tain, ____ My ship __ she's a -

load - ed just __ come __ in from Spain.   3. There are

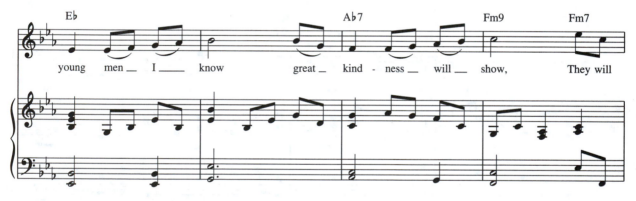

young men __ I __ know   great __ kind - ness __ will __ show,   They will

of - fer __ and __ prof - fer much more than they'll __ owe.   And when

ev - er they can find a ___ maid - en that's kind, ___ With

laugh - ing ___ and ___ chaff - ing they'll change like the wind:

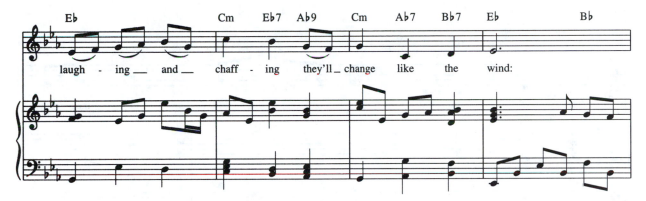

4. But if ev - er I shall ___ prove false ___ to my ___ true ___

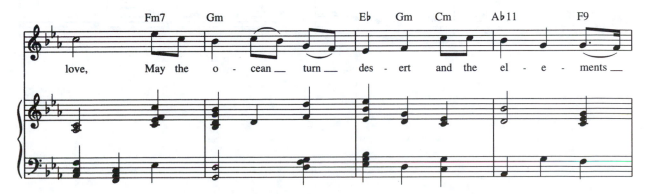

love, May the o - cean ___ turn ___ des - ert and the el - e - ments ___

move; For wher - ev - er I __ shall be, I'll be con - stant to

thee, ___ As a sail - or __ I will jour - ney then come

home __ from the sea. _____

Early One Morning

England
Arranged by
Jean Shackleton

Background and Performance Notes, page 59

leave __ me, How __ could you use __ a __ poor __ maid - en so? Re -

mem - ber the pro - mise you made __ to your loved __ one, Re - mem - ber the

place __ where you vowed __ to be true. Oh, don't de - ceive __ me,

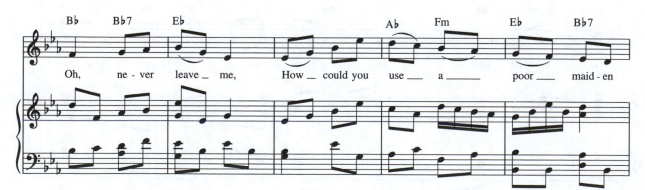

Oh, ne - ver leave __ me, How __ could you use __ a __ poor __ maid - en

Eb   Ab   Eb   Fm7   Bb7   Eb

so?   Oh,

Cm   Fm7   Bb7   Eb

fresh is the gar - land and love - ly the ro - ses I've culled from the

Cm   Fm7   Bb7   Eb   Bb   Bb7   Eb

gar - den to lay at your feet. Oh, don't de - ceive me,

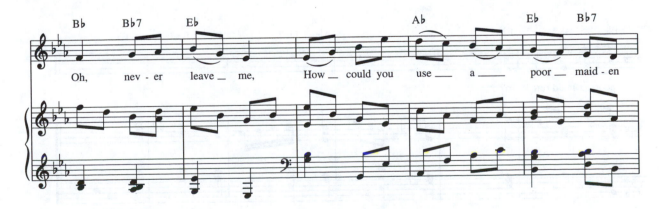

Bb   Bb7   Eb   Ab   Eb   Bb7

Oh, nev - er leave me, How could you use a poor maid - en

93

so? So sang the sweet maid - en, her sad - ness be - wail - ing, Thus

sang the poor maid _ in the val - ley be - low. Oh, don't de -

ceive _ me, oh, nev - er leave _ me, How _ could you use _ a _

poor _ maid - en so?

94

Flow Gently, Sweet Afton

Scotland
Arranged by
Jean Shackleton

Background and Performance Notes, page 62

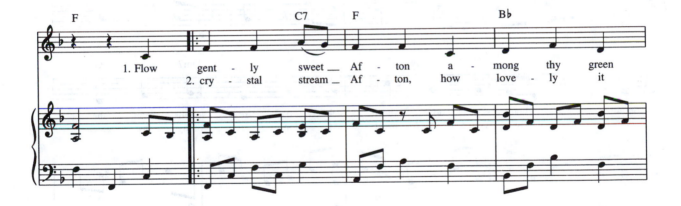

1. Flow gent - ly sweet — Af - ton a - mong thy green
2. cry - stal stream — Af - ton, how love - ly it

braes; Flow gent - ly, I'll sing thee a song in thy
glides, And winds by the cot where my song Mar - y re -

The Juniper Tree

United States
Arranged by
Jean Shackleton

Background and Performance Notes, page 58

O sis - ter Phoe - be, how mer - ry were

we, The night we sat un - der the jun - i - per tree, The jun - i - per

tree, Hi - ho hi - ho, The jun - i - per tree, Hi - ho.

D7   G   D7   G

Put this hat on your head to keep your head warm And one or two

D   G   A7   D   G   D7/G   G

kiss - es will do you no harm, Will do you no harm, I know, I

Em7   Am7   G   Am7   G

know, Will do you no harm, I know.

D   G   D/G

Go choose you a part - ner, go

choose you a one, Go choose you the fair-est that e - ver you

can, Now rise you up, sis - ter, and go, and go, Now

rise you up, sis - ter, and go.

The Kerry Dance

Ireland
Music by
J. L. Malloy
Arranged by
Jean Shackleton

Background and Performance Notes, page 60

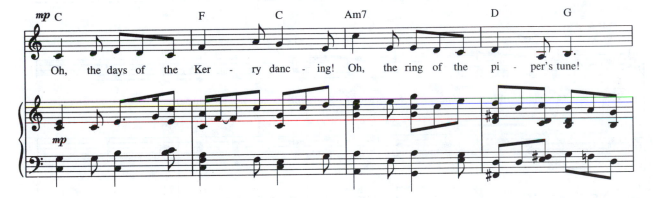

Oh, the days of the Ker - ry danc - ing! Oh, the ring of the pi - per's tune!

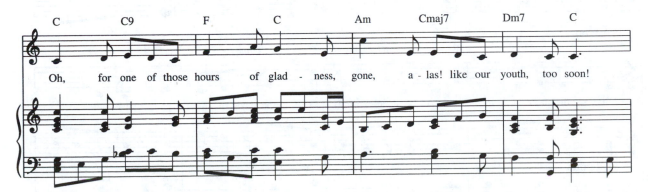

Oh, for one of those hours of glad - ness, gone, a - las! like our youth, too soon!

Oh, for one of those hours of glad - ness, gone, a - las! like our youth, too soon.

My Dearest Love, Why Wilt Thou Ask

Colonial America
Arranged by
Jean Shackleton

Background and Performance Notes, page 58

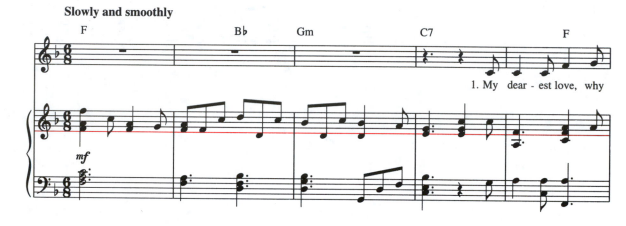

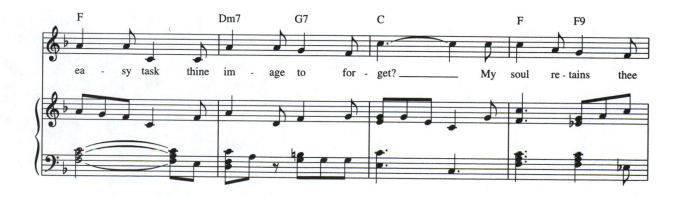

still in sight when thou art far ____ a - way, ____ Thou art my vi - sion

in ____ the night, my wak - ing dream by day.

2. And when the time of

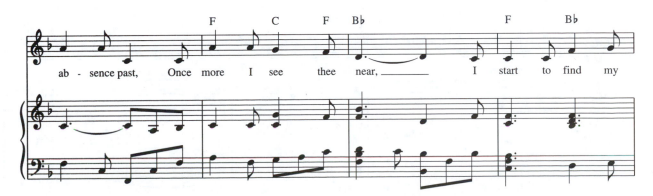

ab - sence past, Once more I see thee near, ____ I start to find my

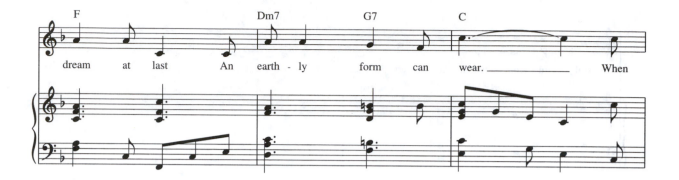

dream at last An earth - ly form can wear. _____ When

far, thou seem'st, some pow'r a - bove To guard my soul __ from harm, _____ When

pre - sent, thou'rt my own __ dear love, That giv'st my life its charm.

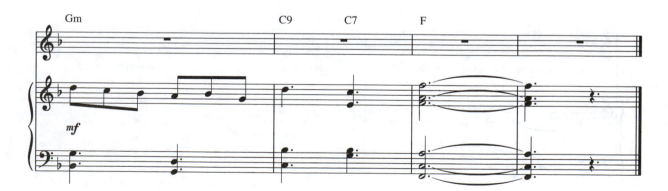

My Love Is like a Red, Red Rose

Scotland
Arranged by
Jean Shackleton

(High Voice)

Background and Performance Notes, page 62

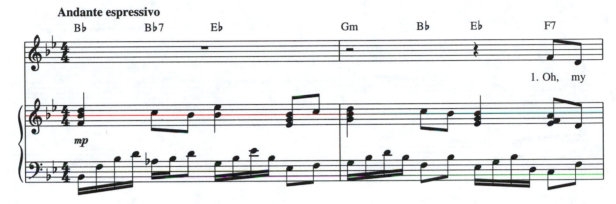

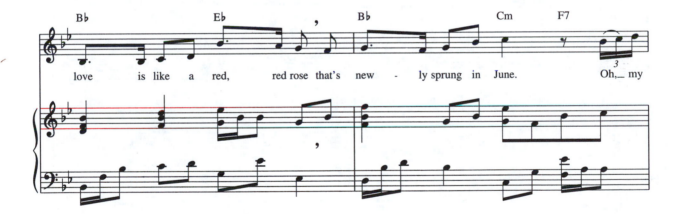

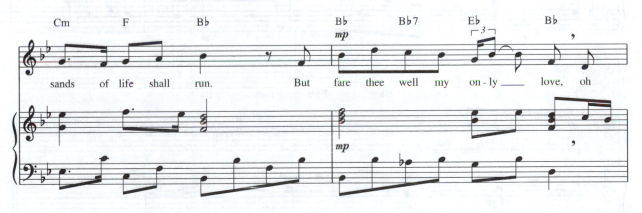

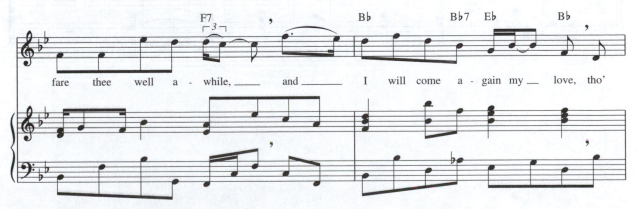

'twere   ten thou - sand mile.   Tho' 'twere   ten thou - sand mile,   my love, tho'

'twere   ten thou - sand mile,   and ___ I   will come a - gain,   my love, tho'

'twere   ten thou - sand mile.

My Love Is like a Red, Red Rose

(Low Voice)

Scotland
Arranged by
Jean Shackleton

Background and Performance Notes, page 62

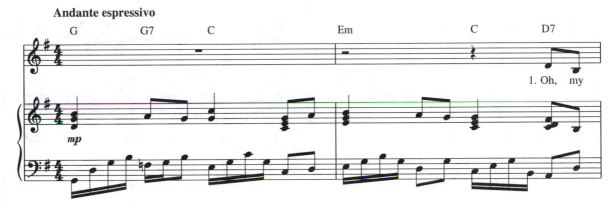

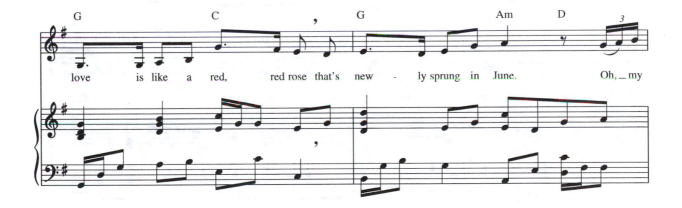

fair art thou my bon-nie __ lass, so deep in love am I, _____ and _____
(lad)

I will love thee still, my dear till all the seas go dry. Till

all the seas go dry, my love, till all the seas go dry, and ____

I will love thee still, my dear, till all the seas go dry.

112

2. Till all the seas go dry my dear, and the rocks melt with the sun. And __ I will love thee still, my dear, while the sands of life shall run. But fare thee well my on - ly __ love, oh fare thee well a - while, __ and __ I will come a - gain my __ love, tho'

113

'twere ten thou - sand mile. Tho' 'twere ten thou - sand mile, my love, tho'

'twere ten thou - sand mile, and ___ I will come a - gain, my love, tho'

'twere ten thou - sand mile.

On the Top of the Hill

South Africa
Arranged by
Jean Shackleton

Background and Performance Notes, page 63

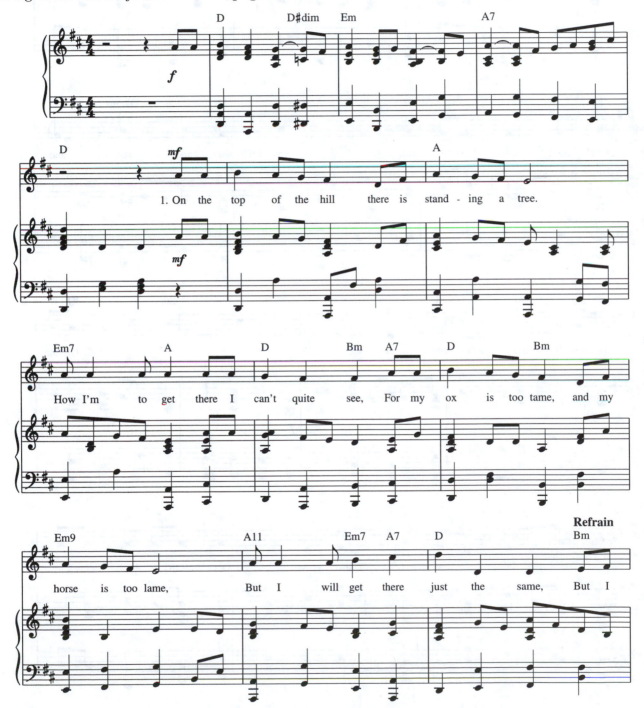

1. On the top of the hill there is stand-ing a tree.

How I'm to get there I can't quite see, For my ox is too tame, and my

horse is too lame, But I will get there just the same, But I

Refrain

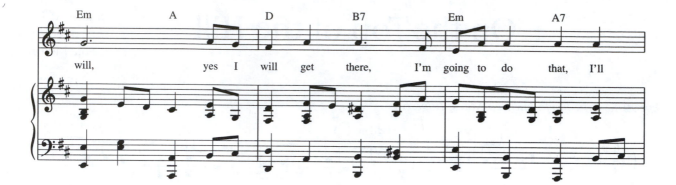

will, yes I will get there, I'm going to do that, I'll

take good care. Yes I will, yes I'll wait and see, and

may-be the tree will _ come to me. 2. On the

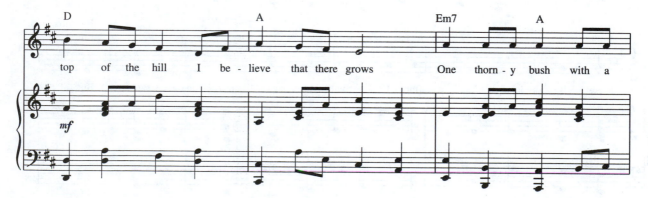

top of the hill I be-lieve that there grows One thorn-y bush with a

116

big white rose. It's too far for a walk, it's too near for a ride;

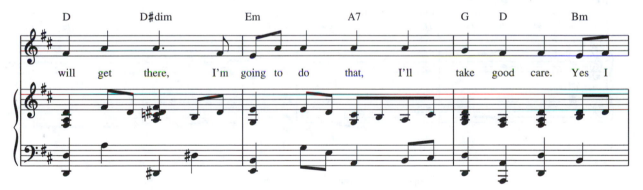

What I'm to do I can't de - cide, but I will, yes I

will get there, I'm going to do that, I'll take good care. Yes I

will, yes I'll wait and see, And may - be the tree will __ come to me.

The River (El Rio)

Peru
Arranged by
Jean Shackleton

Background and Performance Notes, page 62

perfume as it went along its way. 2. Once into the flowing
ri - o, su per - fu - me se lle - vo. Y la flauta del

river a bright shepherd's flute did fall And the river loved the
pas - tor en el ri - o se ca - yo, pu - so se con - ten - to-el

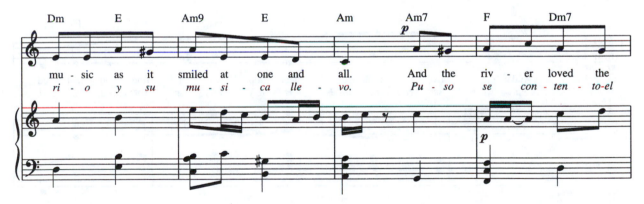

music as it smiled at one and all. And the river loved the
ri - o y su mu - si - ca lle - vo. Pu - so se con - ten - to-el

music as it smiled at one and all.
ri - o y su mu - si - ca lle - vo.

119

Santa Lucia

Italy
Arranged by
Jean Shackleton

Background and Performance Notes, page 60

vite __ us, and as we gent-ly row, all things de - light us.
giv - en, Where smiles cre - a - tion, toil blessed by Heav - en.

Chorus

Hark, how the sail-ors cry joy - ous - ly ech-oes nigh. San - ta __ Lu -

ci - a, San - ta Lu - ci - a. Hark, how the sail-ors cry

joy - ous - ly ech-oes nigh   San - ta___ Lu - ci - a,   San - ta   Lu -

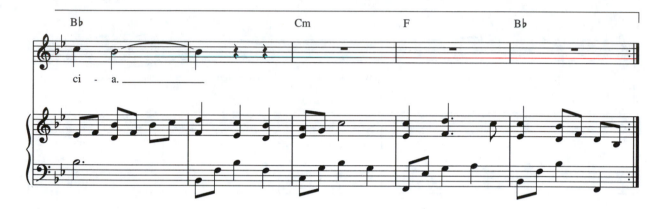

ci - a._____

San-ta___ Lu - ci - a,   San - ta   Lu - ci - a._____

Shady Grove

United States
Arranged by
Jean Shackleton

Background and Performance Notes, page 58

Brightly

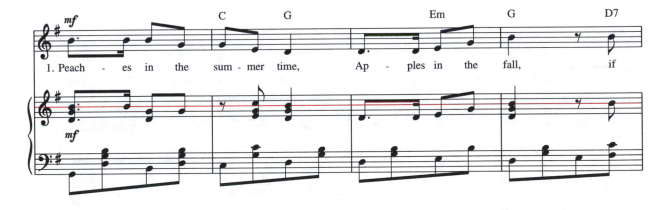

1. Peach - es in the sum - mer time, Ap - ples in the fall, if

I can't get the boy I love, Won't have none at all.
(girl)

Chorus

Shad - y grove, oh my true love, Shad - y grove I know,

Shad - y grove, my true love, I'm bound for the Shad - y grove.

2. Wish I had a ban - jo string, made of gold - en twine, And

ev' - ry time I'd pick on it That boy would sure be mine.
(girl)

126

Chorus

Shad - y grove, oh my true love, Shad - y grove I know,

Shad - y grove, my true love, I'm bound for the Shad - y grove.

3. Fly a-round my blue - eyed boy, Don't you dare be la - zy,
(girl)

The Trees
They Do Grow High

England
Arranged by
Jean Shackleton

Background and Performance Notes, page 59

Allegretto espressivo

1. The trees they do grow

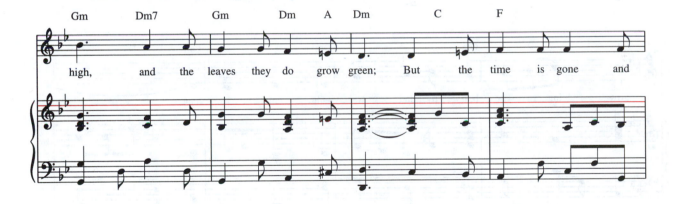

high, and the leaves they do grow green; But the time is gone and

past, my Love, _ that you and I _ have seen, It's a cold win-ter's

night, my Love, when you and I did bide. _____ The bon- ny lad _____ was

young, but a- grow - ing. Grow- ing,

grow - ing _____ The bon- ny lad was young, but a grow -

- ing. _____ 2. O

fa - ther dea - rest fa - ther, I think you've done me harm, ____ You've

mar - ried me to a bon - ny boy, but I fear he is ____ too young. O

daugh - ter, dear - est daugh - ter, but if you stay at home. ____ A

La - dy you ___ shall be while he's grow - ing.

131

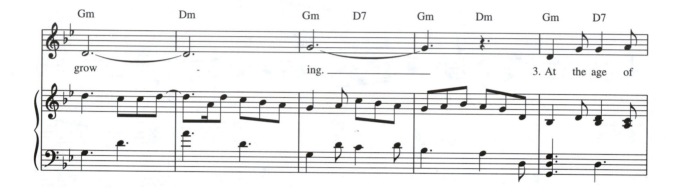

eight - teen his grave was grow-ing green, ___ And so she saw ___ the end of his

grow - ing. Grow - ing, grow - ing ___ And so she saw the

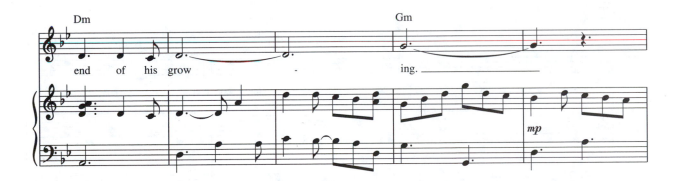

end of his grow - ing. _____

True Lover's Farewell

England
Arranged by
Jean Shackleton

Background and Performance Notes, page 60

Expressively

1. O ___ fare you well, I must be ___ gone, And ___ leave you ___ for a ___ while:

But where - e'er I ___ go, I'll come back a - gain, If I go ten thou - sand miles, my dear, If I

134

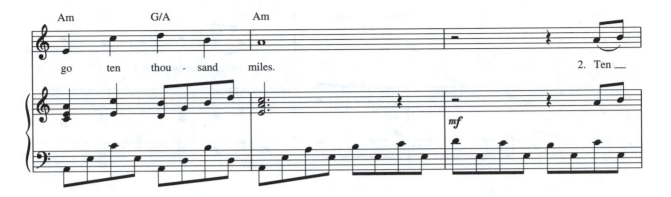

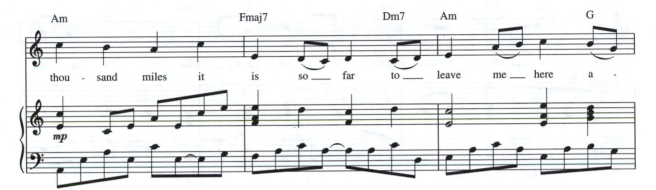

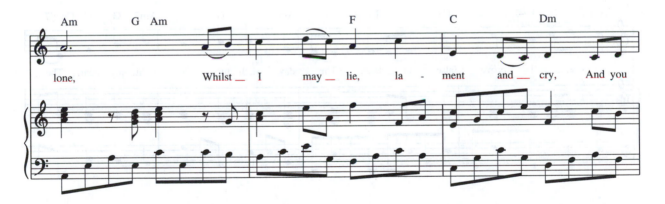

moan.

3. The __ crow that is so

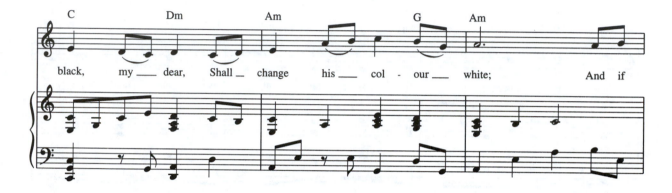

black, my __ dear, Shall __ change his __ col - our __ white; And if

ev - er I prove false __ to __ thee, The __ day shall turn to night, my dear, The __

day shall turn to night.

4. O __ don't you see that

snow - white dove A - perched on yon - der tree, La - ment - ing for her

own true love, As I la - ment for thee, my dear, As

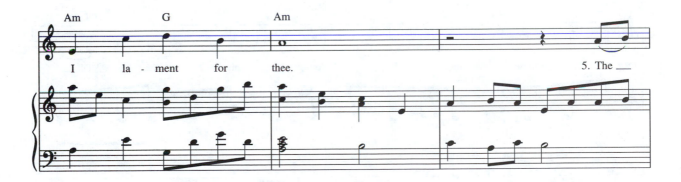

I la - ment for thee. 5. The

riv - ers nev - er will run dry, Nor the

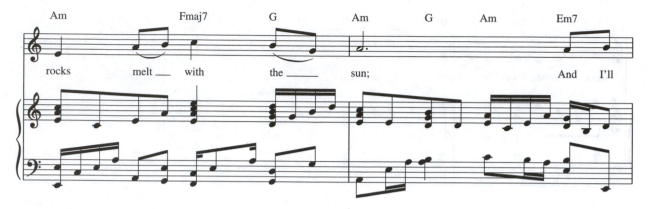

rocks melt __ with the __ sun; And I'll

ne'er prove __ false to the one I __ love Till __

all these things be done, my dear, Till __

all these things be done.

Songs from
Musical Theater

From *Camelot*

Before I Gaze at You Again

Words by
Alan Jay Lerner

Music by
Frederick Loewe

Background and Performance Notes, page 65

tears. Be - fore I gaze at you a - gain Let

hours ___ turn to years. _____ I have so

much for - get - ting to do Be -

fore I try to gaze a - gain at you.

poco accel.

142

Poco più mosso

Stay a-way un-til you cross my mind

Bare-ly once a day; Till the mo-ment I a-

wake and find I can smile and say: That

Tempo I°

I can gaze at you a-gain With-out a blush or

poco rit.

mp dolce

143

qualm, My eyes a-shine like new a-gain, My man-ner poised and calm. Stay far a-way, My love, far a-way. Till I for-get I gazed at you to-day. To-day To-

poco più mosso

day. _____

From *Subways Are for Sleeping*

Words by
Betty Comden and
Adolph Green

Music by
Jule Styne

Comes Once in a Lifetime

Background and Performance Notes, page 65

Who knows what it brings? ___ While the fu - ture waits, ___ the

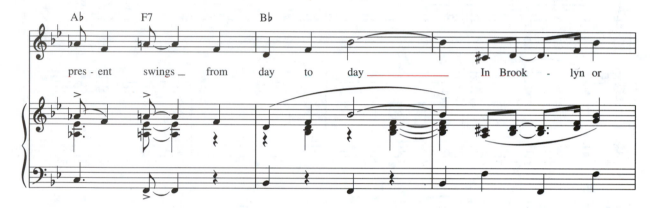

pres - ent swings ___ from day to day _____ In Brook - lyn or

Chi - na 'cross the bay. ___ On - ly once comes this par - tic -

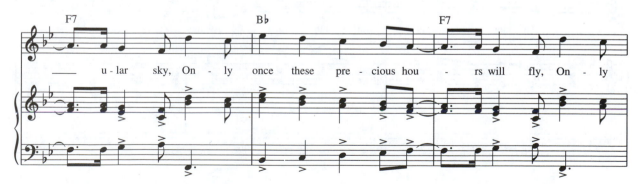

___ u - lar sky, On - ly once these pre - cious hou - rs will fly, On - ly

once in a life - time to-day comes by, ___ So live, live,

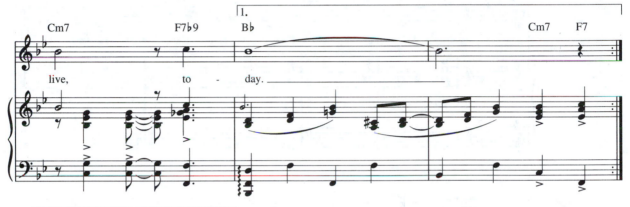

live, to - day. ___

day, ___ Let's live to - day.

149

From *The Secret Garden*

Words by
Marsha Norman

How Could I Ever Know?

Music by
Lucy Simon
Piano arranged by
Michael Kosarin

(High Voice)

Background and Performance Notes, page 65

How_ can I say to go on with-out me? How,_ when I know you still

need me so? How ___ can I say not to dream a-bout me?

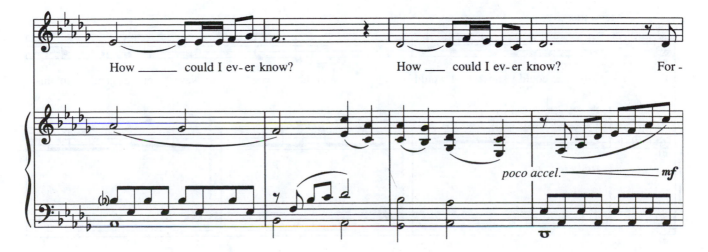

How _____ could I ev-er know? How _____ could I ev-er know? For-

Più passionato

world,   but Oh—   sure   as you breathe,   I   am there   in - side   you.

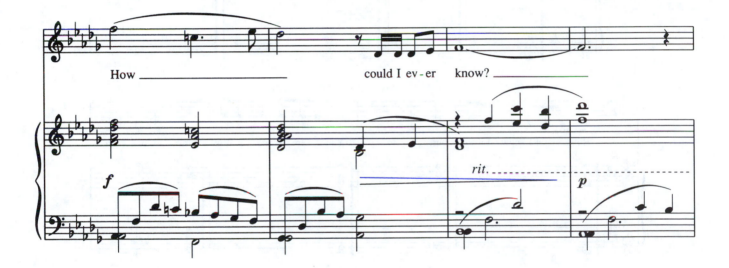

How _____   could I ev - er   know? _____

How _____ could I ev - er   know? _____

153

From *The Secret Garden*

Words by
Marsha Norman

How Could
I Ever Know?

Music by
Lucy Simon
Piano arranged by
Michael Kosarin

(Low Voice)

Background and Performance Notes, page 65

154

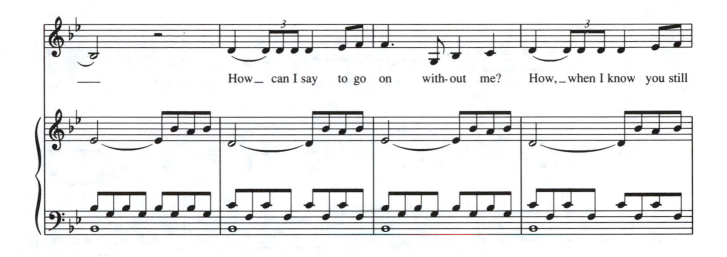

How— can I say to go on with-out me? How,— when I know you still

need me so? How — can I say not to dream a - bout me?

How _____ could I ev-er know? How _____ could I ev-er know? For -

poco accel. _____ *mf*

Più mosso

give me, can you for- give me, and hold me in your heart? And

più mosso

find some new way to love me. Now that we're a - part? ____

rit. _____

Meno mosso

How __ could I know I would nev - er hold you? Nev - er a - gain in this

pp dolcissimo

Più passionato

world, but Oh– sure as you breathe, I am there in-side you.

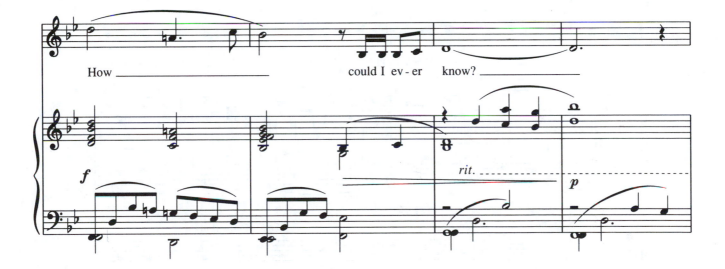

How _____ could I ev - er know? _____

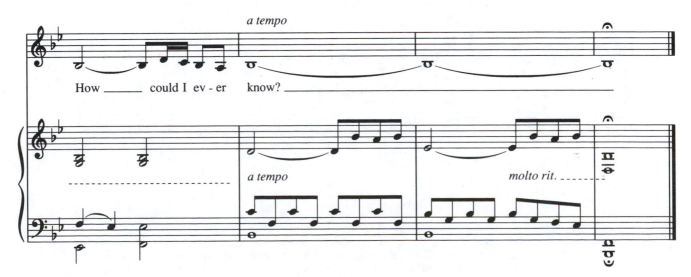

a tempo

How _____ could I ev - er know? _____

molto rit.

From *Love Is a Many-Splendored Thing*

Love Is a Many-Splendored Thing

Words by
Paul Francis
Webster

Music by
Sammy Fain

Background and Performance Notes, page 65

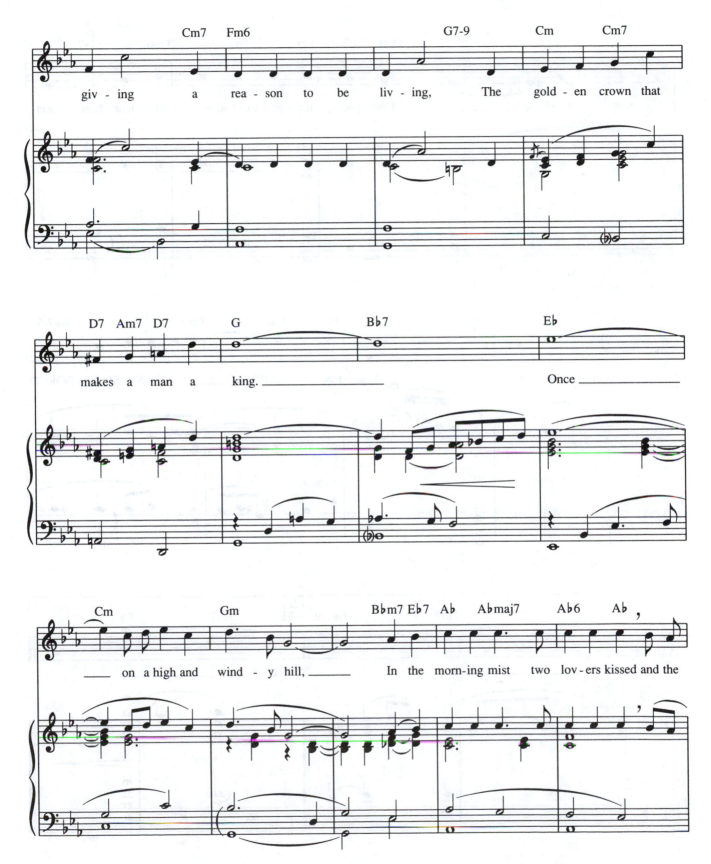

world stood still, _____ Then your fin - gers touched my si - lent heart and

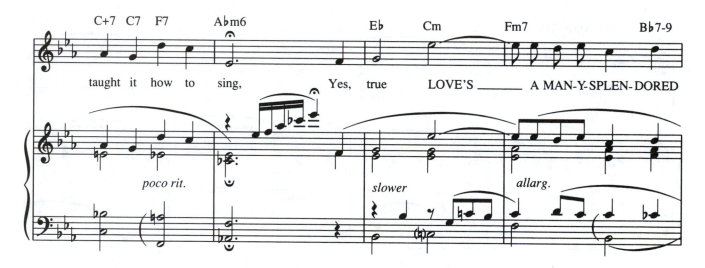

taught it how to sing, Yes, true LOVE'S _____ A MAN-Y-SPLEN-DORED

poco rit.   *slower*   *allarg.*

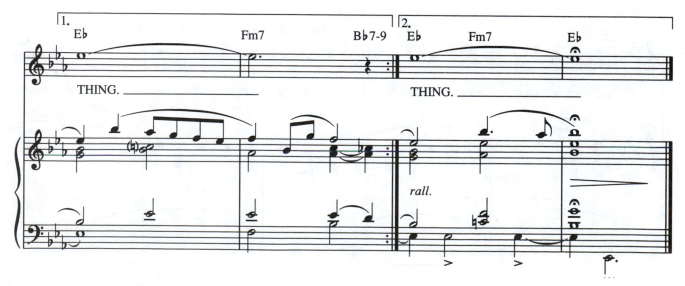

THING. _____   THING. _____

rall.

160

From *The Goldwyn Follies*

Love Walked In

(High Voice)

Words by
Ira Gershwin

Music by
George Gershwin

Background and Performance Notes, page 65

161

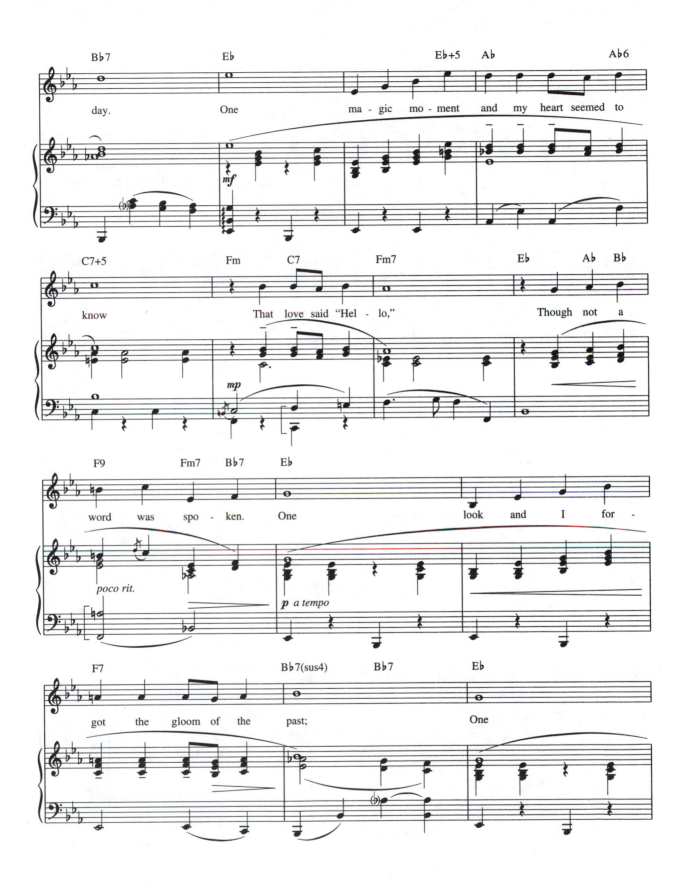

From *The Goldwyn Follies*

Love Walked In

(Low Voice)

Words by
Ira Gershwin

Music by
George Gershwin

Background and Performance Notes, page 65

Refrain: *Slowly, with much expression*

word was spo-ken. One look and I for-got the gloom of the past;

One look and I had found my fu-ture at last,

One look and I had found a world com-plete-ly new, When

Love Walked In with you.
you.

167

From *Breakfast at Tiffany's*

Moon River

Words by
Johnny Mercer

Music by
Henry Mancini

Background and Performance Notes, page 66

169

er the same rain - bow's end _____ wait-in' 'round the

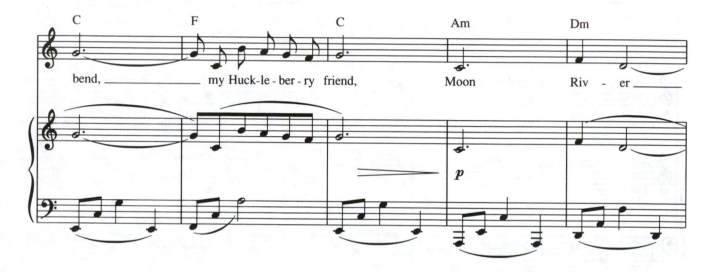

bend, _____ my Huck-le - ber - ry friend, Moon Riv - er _____

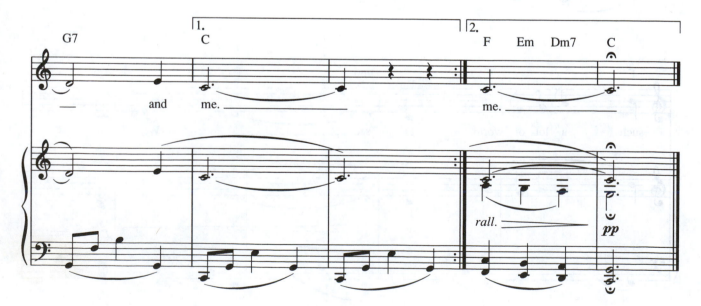

and me. _____ me. _____

rall.

From *Into the Woods*

No One Is Alone

Words and Music by
Stephen Sondheim

Background and Performance Notes, page 66

lone.   Some - times peo - ple leave you ____

Half way through the wood.   Oth - ers may de - ceive you. ____

You de - cide what's good. _____   You de - cide a -

lone,   But no one is a - lone.

dim.   *poco rall.* ——   **p** *a tempo*

marc.   *poco rall.*   *a tempo*

mp

173

Witch-es can be right, Gi-ants can be good, You de-cide what's

right, You de-cide what's good. Just re-mem-ber Some-one is on your side. —

— Some-one else is not. While you're see-ing your side, —

May-be you for-got: They are not a-

175

From *All American*

Once upon a Time

Words by
Lee Adams

Music by
Charles Strouse

Background and Performance Notes, page 66

A Little Faster

the world was sweet-er than we knew,

Ev-'ry-thing was ours, How hap-py we were then;

But some-how Once up-on a time nev-er comes a-

gain.

poco rit.

From *The Sandpiper*

The Shadow of
Your Smile

(High Voice)

Words by
Paul Francis Webster

Music by
Johnny Mandel

Background and Performance Notes, page 66

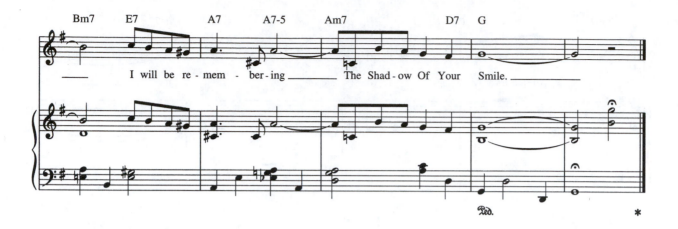

I will be re-mem-ber-ing_____ The Shad-ow Of Your Smile._____

From *The Sandpiper*

The Shadow of
Your Smile

(*Low Voice*)

Words by
Paul Francis Webster

Music by
Johnny Mandel

Background and Performance Notes, page 66

All the love-ly things you are to me.

Our wist-ful lit-tle star was far too high,

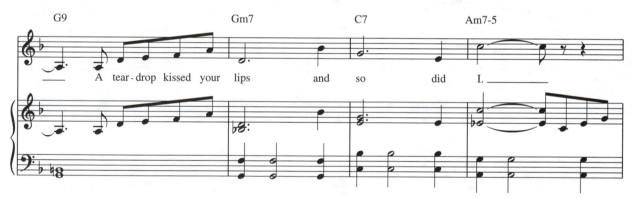

A tear-drop kissed your lips and so did I.

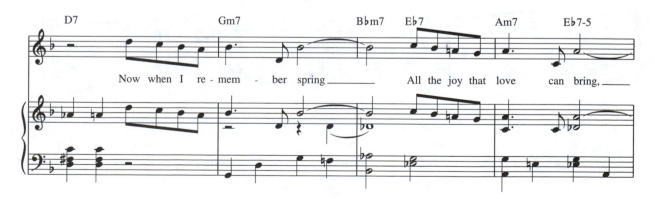

Now when I re-mem - ber spring_____ All the joy that love can bring,_____

184

I will be re-mem - ber-ing _____ The Shad-ow Of Your Smile. _____

Ped.   *

185

From *Woman of the Year*

Words by
Fred Ebb

Sometimes a Day Goes By

Music by
John Kander

Background and Performance Notes, page 67

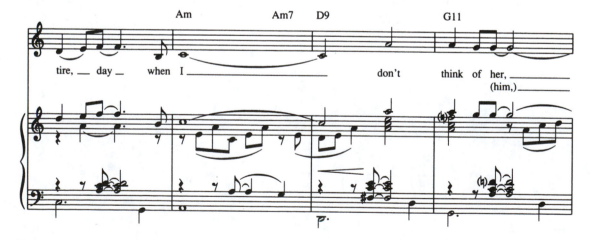

Twen-ty-four hours ___ pass, ___ I look a-round

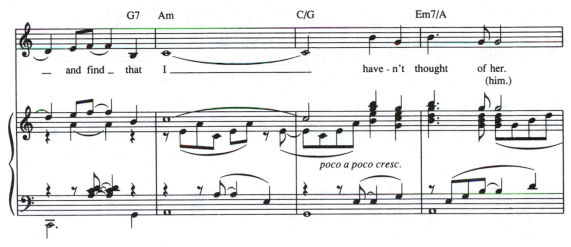

___ and find ___ that I _____ have-n't thought of her.
(him.)

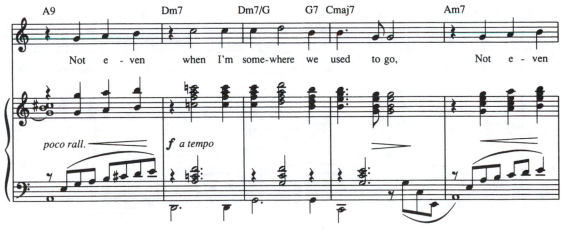

Not e - ven when I'm some-where we used to go, Not e - ven

187

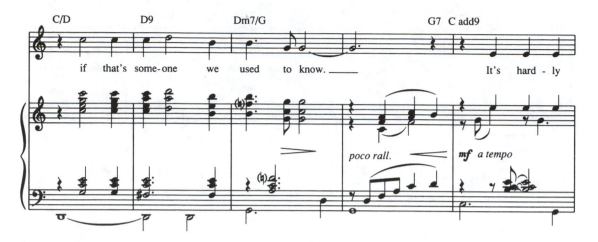

if that's some-one we used to know. _____ It's hard-ly

ev - 'ry-day, _ it's most un-u-su-al, _ in fact,

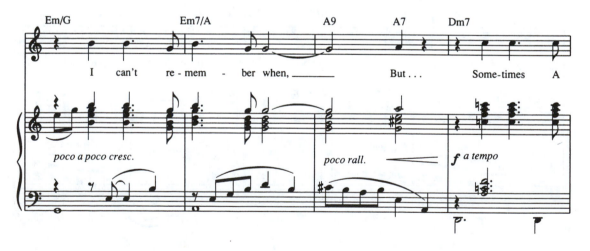

I can't re-mem - ber when, _____ But ... Some-times A

188

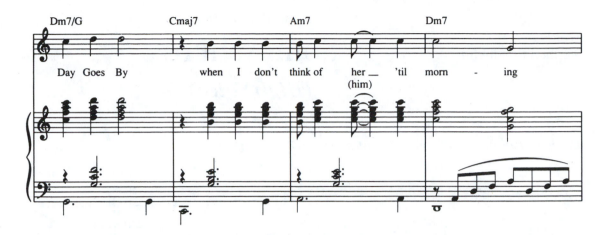

Day Goes By when I don't think of her __ 'til morn - ing
(him)

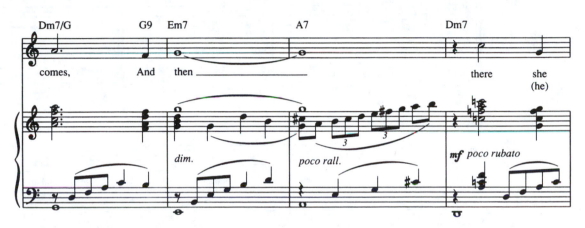

comes, And then __ there she
(he)

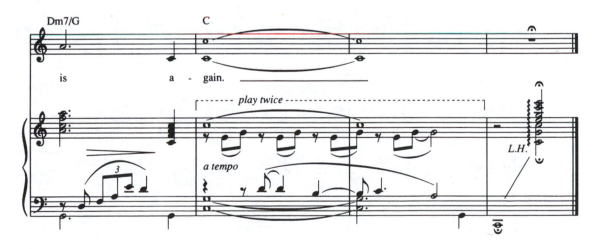

is a - gain. __

From *West Side Story*

Somewhere

(High Voice)

Words by
Stephen Sondheim

Music by
Leonard Bernstein

Background and Performance Notes, page 67

190

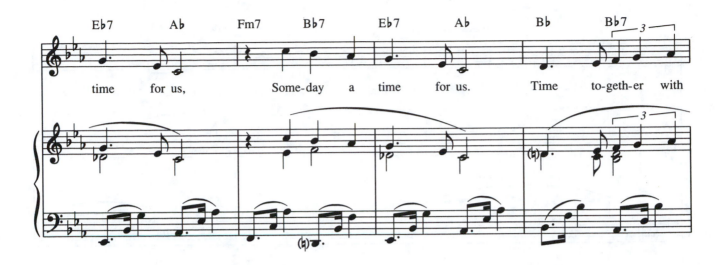

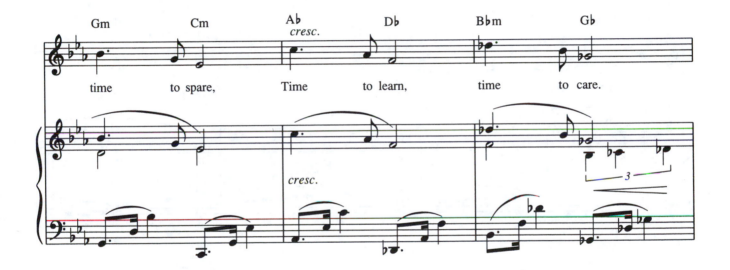

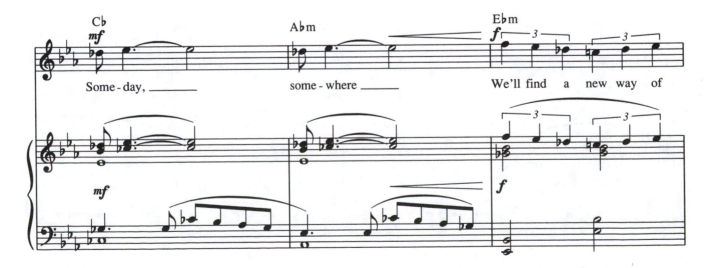

liv - ing,＿＿＿ We'll find a way of for - giv - ing,＿＿＿

some - where. ＿＿＿＿＿＿＿ There's a

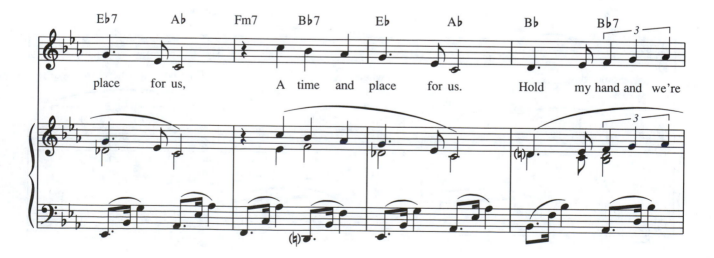

place for us, A time and place for us. Hold my hand and we're

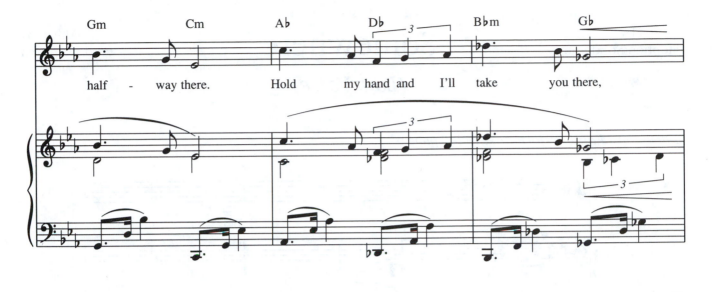

half - way there.   Hold   my hand and   I'll   take   you there,

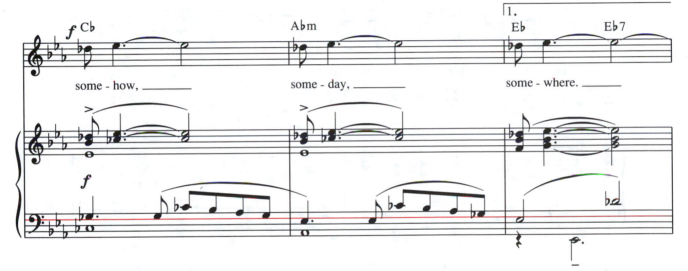

some - how, _____   some - day, _____   some - where. _____

some - where. _____

From *West Side Story*

Somewhere

(Low Voice)

Words by
Stephen Sondheim

Music by
Leonard Bernstein

Background and Performance Notes, page 67

194

time for us, Some-day a time for us. Time to-geth-er with

time to spare, Time to learn, time to care.

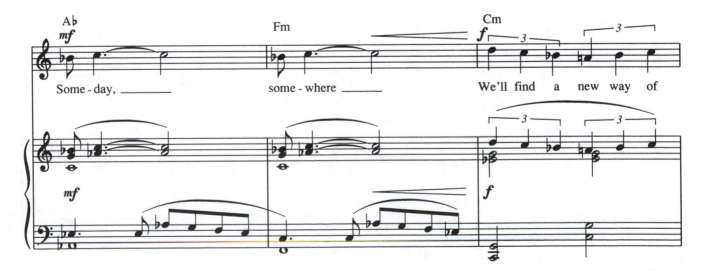

Some-day, ____ some-where ____ We'll find a new way of

liv - ing, _____ We'll find a way of for - giv - ing, _____

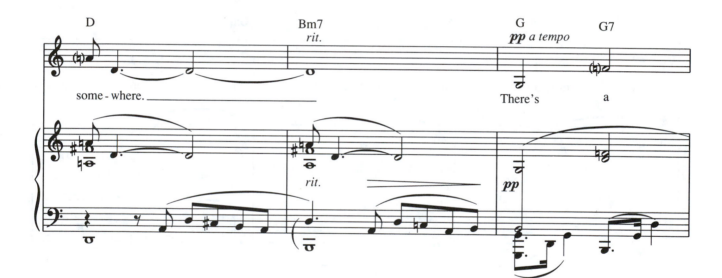

some - where. _____ There's a

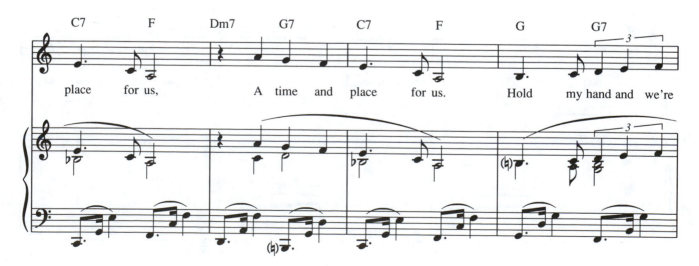

place for us, A time and place for us. Hold my hand and we're

197

From *The Fantasticks*

They Were You

Words by
Tom Jones

Music by
Harvey Schmidt

Background and Performance Notes, page 67

you, they were you, they were you. _____ When the

dance was done, When I went my way, When I

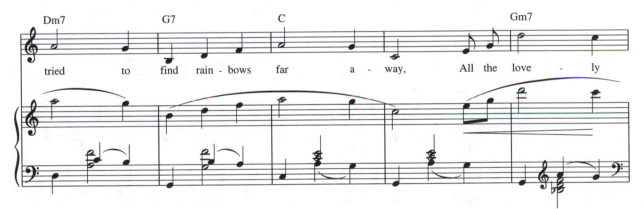

tried to find rain - bows far a - way, All the love - ly

lights seemed to fade from view, They were you, they were you, they were

fan - cy free, Ev -'ry - thing I dared for both you and

me, All my wild - est dreams mul - ti - plied by two, They were

you, they were you, they were you. _____ They were you, they were

you, they were you. _____

rall. e dim.

pp

From *The Happy Ending*

Words by Alan and
Marilyn Bergman

What Are You Doing the Rest of Your Life?

Music by
Michel Legrand

(High Voice)

Background and Performance Notes, page 67

all of my life, _____ Sum-mer, win-ter, spring and fall of my life, _____ All I ev-er will re-

call of my life is all of my life with you!

What Are You Do-ing The you! _____

decresc.

rit. e dim.

From *The Happy Ending*

Words by Alan and Marilyn Bergman

What Are You Doing the Rest of Your Life?

Music by Michel Legrand

(Low Voice)

Background and Performance Notes, page 67

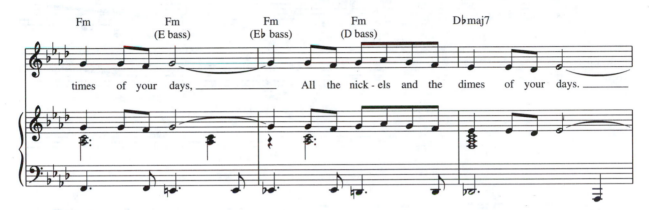

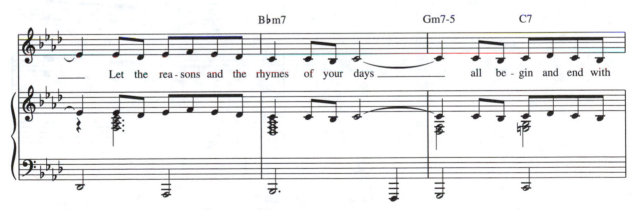

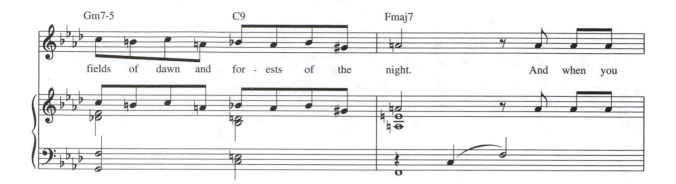

fields of dawn and for-ests of the night. And when you

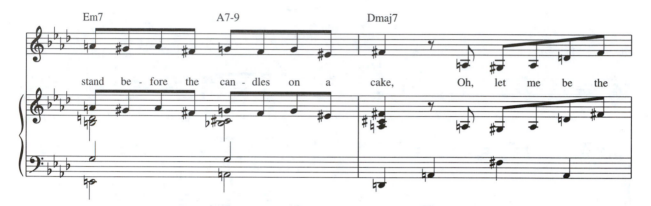

stand be - fore the can - dles on a cake, Oh, let me be the

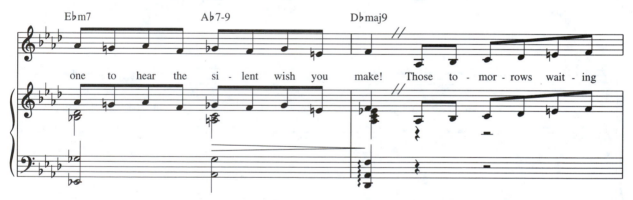

one to hear the si - lent wish you make! Those to - mor - rows wait - ing

deep in your eyes, ___ In the world of love you keep in your eyes, ___

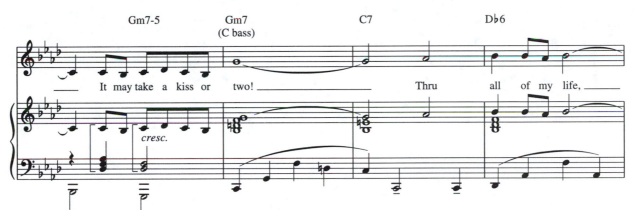

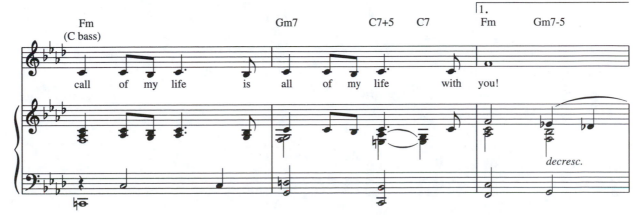

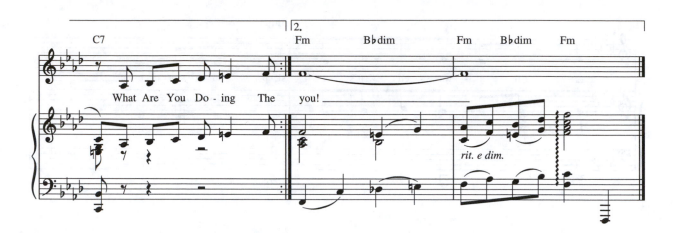

What Are You Do - ing The you!

From *Hook*

When You're Alone

Words by
Leslie Bricusse

Music by
John Williams

Background and Performance Notes, page 68

E

Ev-'ry day must end, but the night's our friend.

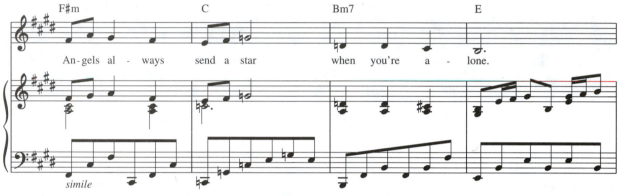

F#m   C   Bm7   E

An-gels al - ways send a star when you're a - lone.

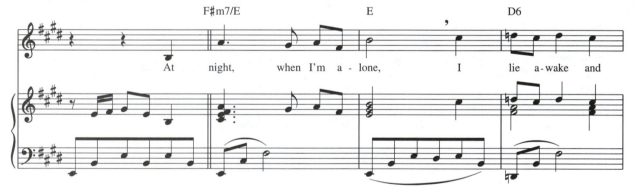

F#m7/E   E   D6

At night, when I'm a - lone, I lie a-wake and

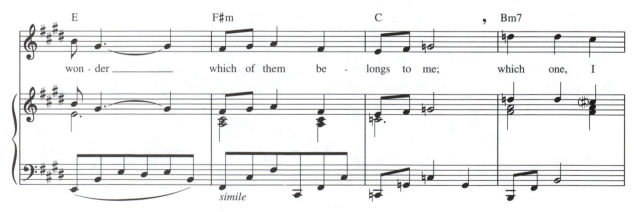

E   F#m   C   Bm7

won - der _____ which of them be - longs to me; which one, I

212

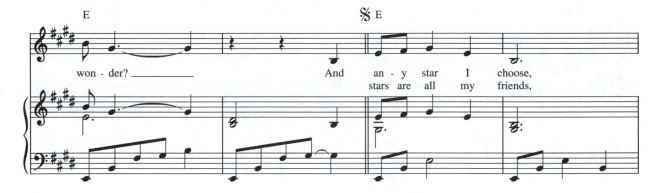

won - der? _____ And an - y star I choose,
stars are all my friends,

watch - es o - ver me. So I know I'm not a - lone,
till the night - time ends. So I know I'm not a - lone,

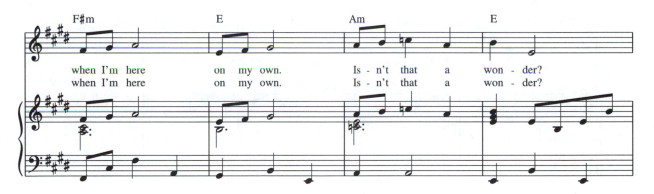

when I'm here on my own. Is - n't that a won - der?
when I'm here on my own. Is - n't that a won - der?

When you're a - lone, you're not a - lone, not
When you're a - lone, you're not a - lone, not

213

real - ly a - lone.

D.S. 𝄋 al Coda ⊕

The

⊕ **Coda**

real - ly a - lone.

Repeat and fade

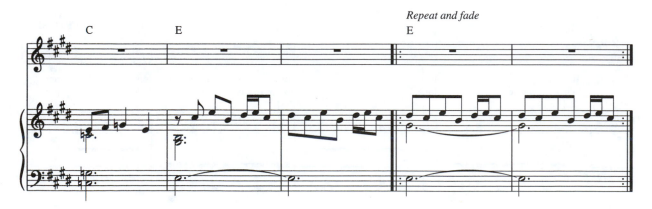

214

From *Babes in Arms*

Where or When

Words by
Lorenz Hart

Music by
Richard Rodgers

Background and Performance Notes, page 68

Refrain (slowly, with very much sentiment)

Art Songs and Arias

American Lullaby

Words and Music by
Gladys Rich

Background and Performance Notes, page 69

keep-ing the wolf from the door.

Nurs-ie will raise the win-dow shade high, So you can see the

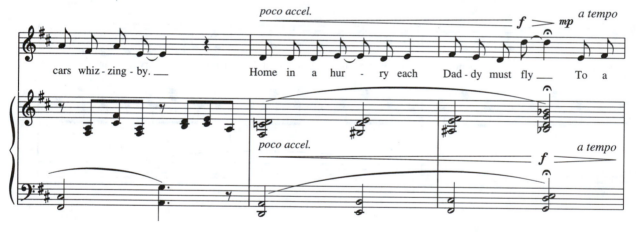

cars whiz-zing by. Home in a hur-ry each Dad-dy must fly To a

poco accel. *f* > *mp* *a tempo*

ba - by like you.

Hush - a - bye, you sweet little ba - by, And

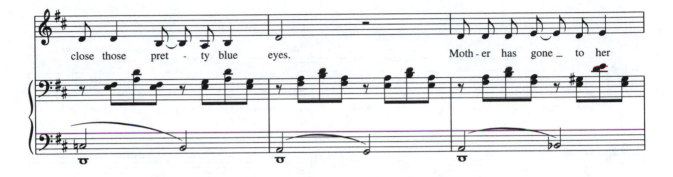

close those pret - ty blue eyes. Moth - er has gone to her

week - ly bridge par - ty To get her wee ba - by the prize.

Nurs - ie will turn the ra - di - o on,

So you can hear ___ a sleep-y-time song, ___

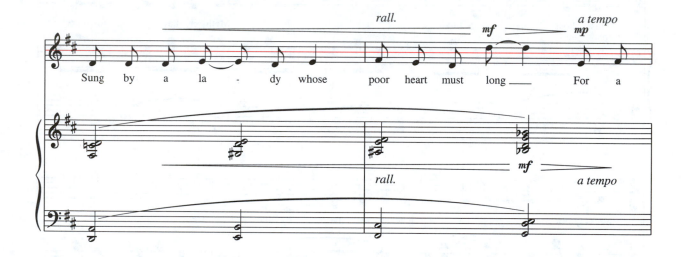

Sung by a la - dy whose poor heart must long ___ For a

ba - by like you! ___

dim. e rall.

Piano arrangement
from the original by
Roy S. Stoughton

Beneath a Weeping Willow's Shade

Words and Music by
Francis Hopkinson
(1737–1791)

Background and Performance Notes, page 69

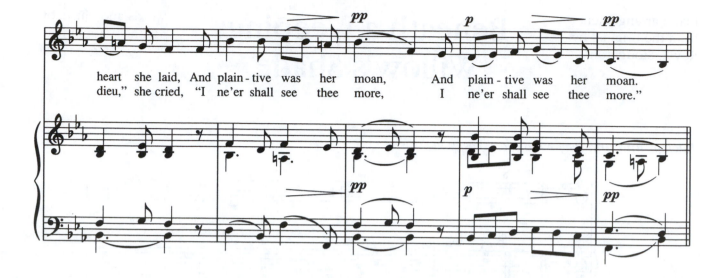

heart she laid, And plain - tive was her moan, And plain - tive was her moan.
dieu," she cried, "I ne'er shall see thee more, I ne'er shall see thee more."

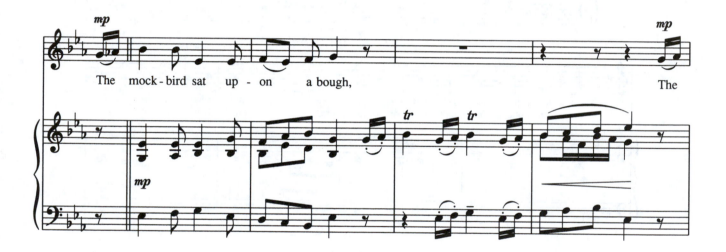

The mock - bird sat up - on a bough, The

mock - bird sat up - on a bough And lis - ten'd to her lay, Then

to the dis - tant hills he bore The dul - cet notes a - way, Then

to the dis - tant hills he bore The dul - cet notes a - way, The

dul - cet notes a - way, The dul - cet notes a - way. way.

Bright Is the Ring of Words

(High Voice)

Background and Performance Notes, page 70

Moderato risoluto.

Bright is the ring of words ____ When the right man rings them, Fair the fall of songs ____ When the sing - er sings them. Still they are ca - rolled and said— On wings they are car - ried ____

After the sing - er is dead And the mak - er bur - ied. _____ Low as the sing - er lies _____ In the field of hea - ther, Songs of his fash - ion bring The swains to - geth - er.

poco rit.

229

And when the west is red With the sun - set em - - - - bers, The lov - - er lin - - gers and sings, ____ And the maid re - mem - - bers.

la melodia ben marcato.

pp molto più lento.

colla voce.

pp molto più lento.

rall.

230

Words by
R. L. Stevenson

Bright Is the
Ring of Words

(Low Voice)

Music by Ralph
Vaughan Williams
(1872–1958)

Background and Performance Notes, page 70

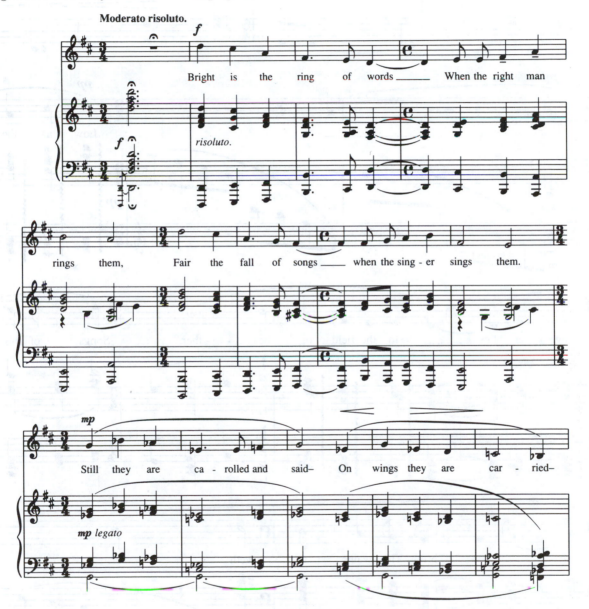

And when the west is red With the

sun - set em - - - - bers,

The lov - er lin - - gers and

sings, _____ And the maid - re - mem - - bers.

la melodia ben marcato.

p

pp molto più lento.

colla voce.

pp molto più lento.

rall.

Words by
Robert Hillyer

Early in the Morning

Music by
Ned Rorem
(1923 –)

Background and Performance Notes, page 70

234

green-er - y like scen-er - y, Rue Fran - çois Pre - mier.

They were hos-ing the hot pave-ment With a dash of flash-ing spray__ And a

smell of sum - mer show - ers When the dust is drenched a - way.__ Un-der green-er - y like

scen-er - y, Rue Fran - çois Pre - mier,__

I was twen-ty and a lov-er And in

Par-a-dise to stay, Ver-y ear-ly in the morn-ing Of a love-ly sum-mer

day.

Words by
Henry Heveningham

If music be
the food of love

(High Voice)

Music by
Henry Purcell

Background and Performance Notes, page 70

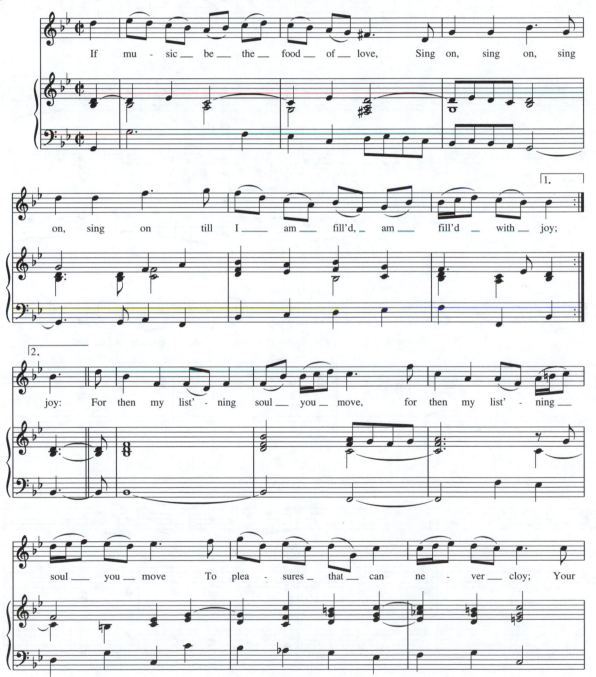

eyes, your mien, your tongue de-clare That you are mu - sic e-v'ry -

where; Your eyes, your mien, your tongue de-clare That you are mu -

Second stanza

- sic e-v'ry - where. Plea-sures in-vade both eye and ear, So

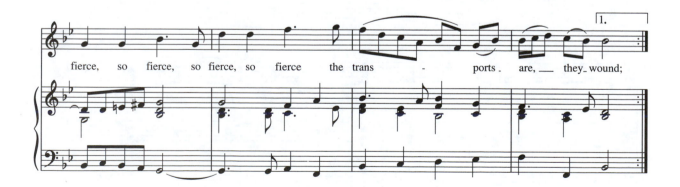

fierce, so fierce, so fierce, so fierce the trans - ports are, they wound;

wound; And all my sen - ses feast - ed are, and all my sen - ses _____ feast - ed _ are, Tho'

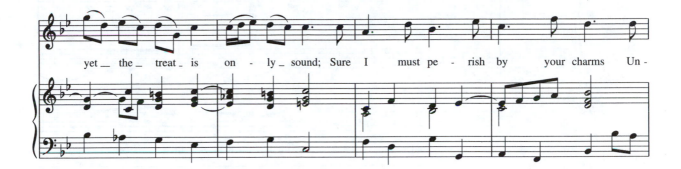

yet _ the _ treat _ is on - ly _ sound; Sure I must pe - rish by your charms Un-

less you save _____ me _ in your _ arms; Sure I must pe - rish

by your charms Un - less you save _____ me _ in your _ arms.

Words by
Henry Heveningham

If music be
the food of love

(Low Voice)

Music by
Henry Purcell

Background and Performance Notes, page 70

eyes, your mien, your tongue de-clare That you are mu - sic e - v'ry -

where; Your eyes, your mien, your tongue de-clare That you are mu -

Second stanza

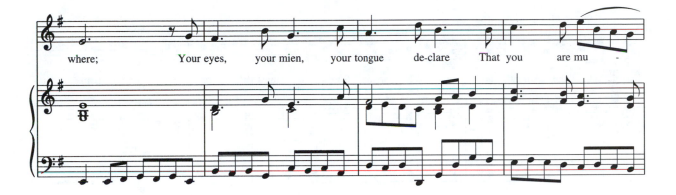

- sic e - v'ry - where. Plea - sures in - vade both eye and ear, So

1.

fierce, so fierce, so fierce, so fierce the trans - ports are, they wound;

wound; And all my sen - ses feast - ed _ are, and all my sen - ses ___ feast - ed _ are, Tho'

yet _ the _ treat _ is on - ly _ sound; Sure I must pe - rish by your charms Un -

less you save _____ me _ in your _ arms; Sure I must pe - rish

by your charms Un - less you save _____ me _ in your _ arms.

Words by
Friedrich Rückert

Lachen und Weinen

(High Voice)

Music by
Franz Schubert

Background and Performance Notes, page 70

Lachen und Weinen	Laughter and tears
Zu jeglicher Stunde	At all hours
Ruht bei der Lieb'	Can have so many causes
Auf so mancherlei Grunde.	When one is in love.
Morgens lacht' ich vor Lust,	In the morning I laughed with pleasure,
Und warum ich nun weine	And why I now weep
Bei des Abendes Scheine,	In the evening light,
Ist mir selb' nicht bewußt.	I myself do not know.
Weinen und Lachen	Tears and laughter
Zu jeglicher Stunde	At all hours
Ruht bei der Lieb'	Can have so many causes
Auf so mancherlei Grunde.	When one is in love.
Abends weint' ich vor Schmerz;	In the evening I was weeping with grief;
Und warum du erwachen	And how can you wake
Kannst am Morgen mit Lachen,	In the morning with laughter,
Muß ich dich fragen, o Herz!	I must ask you, my heart!

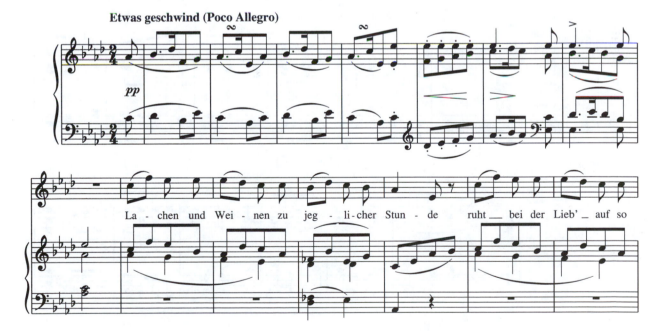

man - cher -lei Grun - de. Mor - gens lacht' ich vor Lust, _____

und wa - rum ich nun wei - ne bei des A - ben-des Schei - ne,

ruhiger

decresc.

dimin.

ist mir selb'_ nicht be - wusst, ist mir selb'_ nicht be - wusst.

a tempo

a tempo

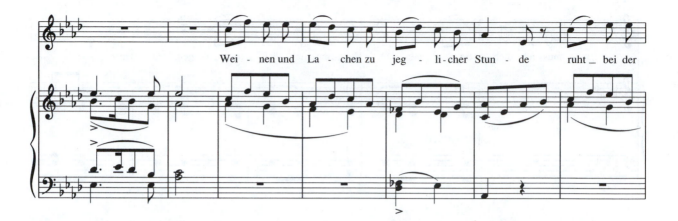

Wei - nen und La - chen zu jeg - li - cher Stun - de ruht _ bei der

Lieb' _ auf so man - cher - lei Grun - de. A - bends weint' ich vor Schmerz; ___

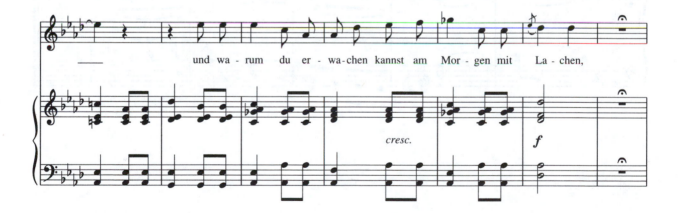

___ und wa - rum du er - wa - chen kannst am Mor - gen mit La - chen,

cresc.   f

muss ich dich fra - gen, O Herz, muss ich dich fra - gen, O Herz.

Words by
Friedrich Rückert

Lachen und Weinen

(Low Voice)

Music by
Franz Schubert

Background and Performance Notes, page 70

Lachen und Weinen	Laughter and tears
Zu jeglicher Stunde	At all hours
Ruht bei der Lieb'	Can have so many causes
Auf so mancherlei Grunde.	When one is in love.
Morgens lacht' ich vor Lust,	In the morning I laughed with pleasure,
Und warum ich nun weine	And why I now weep
Bei des Abendes Scheine,	In the evening light,
Ist mir selb' nicht bewußt.	I myself do not know.
Weinen und Lachen	Tears and laughter
Zu jeglicher Stunde	At all hours
Ruht bei der Lieb'	Can have so many causes
Auf so mancherlei Grunde.	When one is in love.
Abends weint' ich vor Schmerz;	In the evening I was weeping with grief;
Und warum du erwachen	And how can you wake
Kannst am Morgen mit Lachen,	In the morning with laughter,
Muß ich dich fragen, o Herz!	I must ask you, my heart!

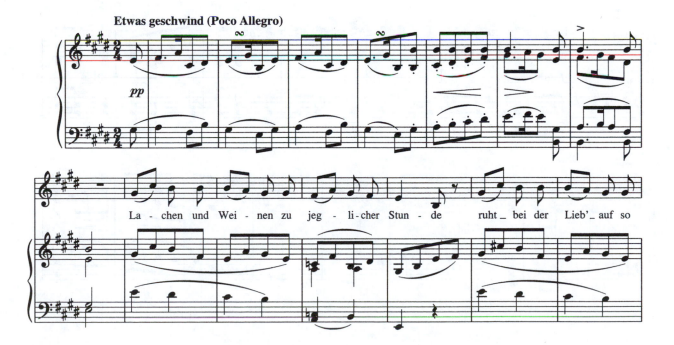

man - cher-lei Grun - de. Mor - gens lacht' ich vor Lust, _____

ruhiger

und wa - rum ich nun wei - ne bei des A - ben-des Schei - ne,

a tempo

ist mir selb'_ nicht be - wusst, ist mir selb'_ nicht be - wusst.

Wei - nen und La - chen zu jeg - li - cher Stun - de ruht _ bei der

Lieb' _ auf so man - cher-lei Grun - de. A - bends weint' _ ich vor Schmerz; _

_ und wa - rum du er - wa-chen kannst am Mor - gen mit La - chen,

cresc.

f

muss ich dich fra - gen, O Herz, muss ich dich fra - gen, O Herz.

Translation by
Metche Franke

Words and Music by
Clara Schumann
(1819–1896)

Liebst du um Schönheit

(High Voice)

Background and Performance Notes, page 71

Liebst du um Schönheit	Do you love beauty?
o nicht mich liebe!	Oh do not love me!
Liebe die Sonne,	Love thou the sun
sie trägt gold'nes Haar!	who wears her golden hair!
Liebst du um Jugend,	Do you love youth?
o nicht mich liebe!	Oh do not love me!
Liebe den Frühling,	Love thou the Spring,
der jung ist jedes Jahr!	it is young every year!
Liebst du um Schätze,	Do you love riches?
o nicht mich liebe!	Oh do not love me!
Liebe die Meerfrau,	Love thou the mermaid (ocean),
sie hat viel Perlen klar.	she (it) has many pearls!
Liebst du um Liebe,	Do you love love?
o ja mich liebe!	Oh yes, then love me!
liebe mich immer,	Love me always,
dich lieb ich immerdar!	I will always love you!

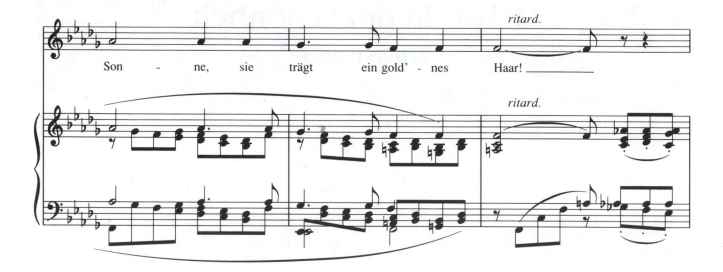

ritard.

Son - ne, sie trägt ein gold' - nes Haar! _____

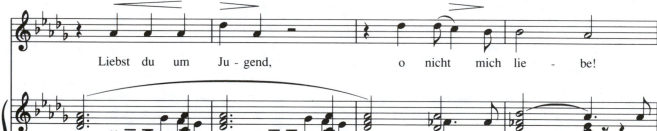

Liebst du um Ju - gend, o nicht mich lie - be!

Lie - be den Früh - ling, der jung ist je - des

Jahr! Liebst du um Schä - tze, o nicht __ mich

lie - be! Lie - be die Meer - frau, sie hat viel Per - len

Bewegter.

klar! Liebst du um Lie - be, o ja __ mich

253

lie - be!   Liebst du um Lie - be,   o ja mich lie - be,

lie - be mich im - mer, dich lieb' ich im - - mer - dar! _____

Liebst du um Schönheit

(Low Voice)

Background and Performance Notes, page 71

Liebst du um Schönheit	Do you love beauty?
o nicht mich liebe!	Oh do not love me!
Liebe die Sonne,	Love thou the sun
sie trägt gold'nes Haar!	who wears her golden hair!
Liebst du um Jugend,	Do you love youth?
o nicht mich liebe!	Oh do not love me!
Liebe den Frühling,	Love thou the Spring,
der jung ist jedes Jahr!	it is young every year!
Liebst du um Schätze,	Do you love riches?
o nicht mich liebe!	Oh do not love me!
Liebe die Meerfrau,	Love thou the mermaid (ocean),
sie hat viel Perlen klar.	she (it) has many pearls!
Liebst du um Liebe,	Do you love love?
o ja mich liebe!	Oh yes, then love me!
liebe mich immer,	Love me always,
dich lieb ich immerdar!	I will always love you!

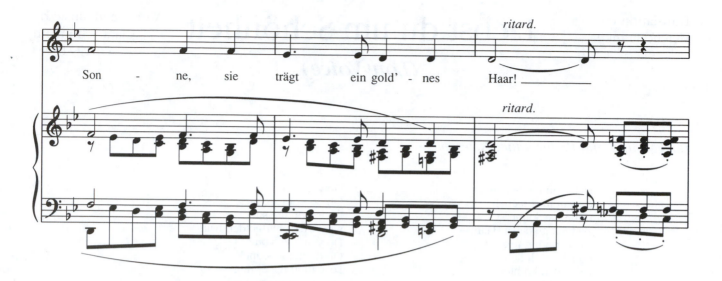

Son - ne, sie trägt ein gold' - nes Haar!

Liebst du um Ju - gend, o nicht mich lie - be!

Lie - be den Früh - ling, der jung ist je - des

Jahr! Liebst du um Schä - tze, o nicht _ mich

lie - be! Lie - be die Meer - frau, sie hat viel Per - len

Bewegter.

klar! Liebst du um Lie - be, o ja _ mich

lie - be! Liebst du um Lie - be, o ja mich lie - be,

lie - be mich im - mer, dich lieb' ich im - - mer - dar! _____

Words by
Charles Coffey
(d. 1745)

Long Have I Been with Grief Opprest

(High Voice)

Background and Performance Notes, page 71

Li - ber - ty. Our __ Life is __ oft with Clouds __ o'er - cast, As __

are _____ the bright - est __ Sum - mer __ Days, But __ when those __ Shad - ows

all are past, The __ Sun __ shoots __ forth __ en - liv'n - ing Rays.

Words by
Charles Coffey
(d. 1745)

Long Have I Been with Grief Opprest

(Low Voice)

Unidentified

Background and Performance Notes, page 71

Long _ have I ____ been with

Grief _ op - prest, Each Night o'er - whelms _ with _ Mi - ser - y, But _

now I ____ shall lie down and rest, And _ rise _ each _ Morn - ing to

261

Li - ber - ty. Our __ Life is __ oft with Clouds __ o'er - cast, As __

are __ the bright - est __ Sum - mer __ Days, But __ when those __ Shad - ows

all are past, The __ Sun __ shoots __ forth __ en - liv'n - ing Rays.

Loveliest of Trees

Background and Performance Notes, page 71

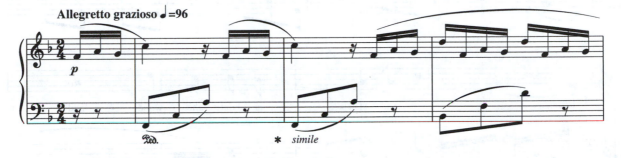

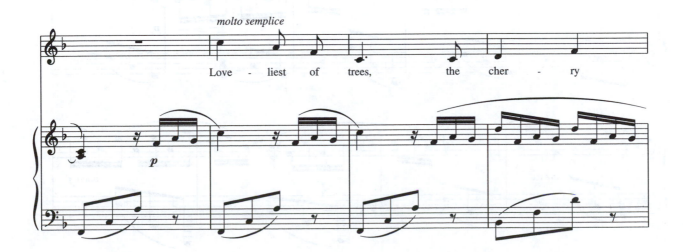

now   Is   hung   with   bloom   a - long   the

bough, _____   And   stands _____   a - bout   the   wood - land

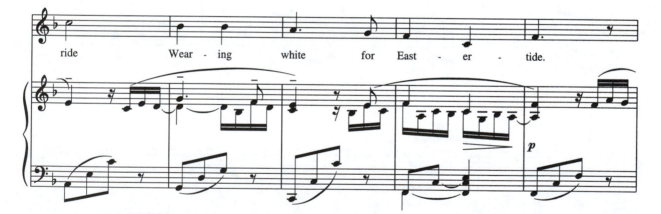

ride   Wear - ing   white   for   East - er - tide.

Now, of my three - score years and ten.

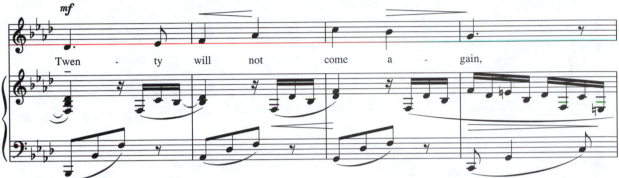

Twen - ty will not come a - gain,

And take from sev - en - ty springs a

score, It on - ly leaves me

fif - ty more. _____

poco f

pp subito

pp

And since to look at things in bloom

tranquillo e sempre pp

*

Fif - ty springs are lit - tle room,

pp

A - bout the wood - lands I will go To

pp

mp

see the cher - ry hung _____ with

snow. _____

267

O cessate di piagarmi

Background and Performance Notes, page 71

O cessate di piagarmi,
o lasciatemi morir,
o lasciatemi morir.
Luc'ingrate, dispietate,
luc'ingrate, dispietate,
più del gelo e più del marmi
fredde e sorde a' miei martir,
fredde e sorde a' miei martir.
O cessate di piagarmi,
o lasciatemi morir,
o lasciatemi morir.

O no longer seek to pain me,
Or give o'er, and let me die,
Or give o'er, and let me die.
Eyes so fateful, so ungrateful,
Eyes so fateful, so ungrateful;
Ice nor stone could so disdain me,
Nor so coldly hear my cry,
Nor so coldly hear my cry.
Or no longer seek to pain me,
Or give o'er, and let me die,
Or give o'er, and let me die.

English lyric by
Thomas W. van Ess

Qué Pronto
(Love's Short Memory)

Harmonized by
Manuel Ponce
(1882–1948)

(High Voice)

Background and Performance Notes, page 71

Qué pronto se te olvidó	How quickly it slipped your mind,
El falso juramento,	How false the oath you took with me!
Que sin necesidad,	You lavished all your love,
A mi amor le prodigaste.	And you said you truly loved me.
Qué pronto se te olvidó,	How quickly it slipped your mind,
Que con pasión me amaste	O but you spoke with passion;
Todo fué un sueño	It all was false illusion,
todo se volvió ilusión.	All was but a dream.
Que, que mal hiciste	How you hurt me badly,
con que me hubieras amado,	When you really might have loved me,
Ofendiste a un dios,	You slighted a god,
Fiel y verdadero.	True and faithful ever.
Qué pronto se te olvidó,	How quickly it slipped your mind,
Que fui tu amor primero,	I was your only lover,
Todo fué un sueño	It all was false illusion,
todo se volvió ilusión.	All was but a dream.

mor   le pro - di - gas - te.____   Qué pron - to se te ol - vi - dó,____
said   you tru - ly loved me.____   How quick - ly   it slipped   your   mind,____

Que con pa - sión   me a - mas - te   To - do   fué un
O but you spoke   with pas - sion;   It all   was

rit.   a tempo

sue - ño to - do se   vol - vió i - lu - sion.____
false   il - lu - sion, All   was but   a   dream.____

1.   2.   rall.   a tempo

Que mal   hi - cis - te ____   con que
You hurt   me bad - ly ____   when you

rall.   a tempo

me hu - bie - ras a - ma - do, _____ O - fen - dis - te aun
real - ly might have loved me, _____ You slight - ed a

dios Fiel y ver - da - de - ro. _____
god, True and faith - ful ev - er. _____

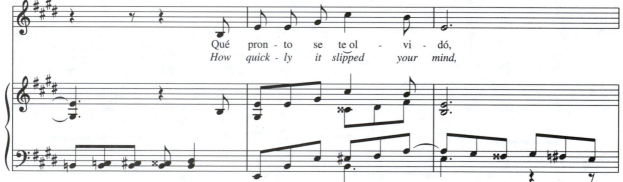

Qué pron - to se te ol - vi - dó,
How quick - ly it slipped your mind,

Que fui tu a - mor pri - me - ro, _____ To - do fué un
I was your on - ly lov - er, _____ It all was

rall.   a tempo

sue - ño to - do se vol - vió i - lu - sion. _____

false   il - lu - sion, All   was but   a   dream. _____

273

English lyric by
Thomas W. van Ess

Qué Pronto
(Love's Short Memory)

(Low Voice)

Harmonized by
Manuel Ponce
(1882–1948)

Background and Performance Notes, page 71

Qué pronto se te olvidó	How quickly it slipped your mind,
El falso juramento,	How false the oath you took with me!
Que sin necesidad,	You lavished all your love,
A mi amor le prodigaste.	And you said you truly loved me.
Qué pronto se te olvidó,	How quickly it slipped your mind,
Que con pasión me amaste	O but you spoke with passion;
Todo fué un sueño	It all was false illusion,
todo se volvió ilusion.	All was but a dream.
Que, que mal hiciste	How you hurt me badly,
con que me hubieras amado,	When you really might have loved me,
Ofendiste a un dios,	You slighted a god,
Fiel y verdadero.	True and faithful ever.
Qué pronto se te olvidó,	How quickly it slipped your mind,
Que fui tu amor primero,	I was your only lover,
Todo fué un sueño	It all was false illusion,
todo se volvió ilusion.	All was but a dream.

mor le pro - di - gas - te. _____ Qué pron - to se te ol - vi - dó, _____
said you tru - ly loved me. _____ How quick - ly it slipped your mind, _____

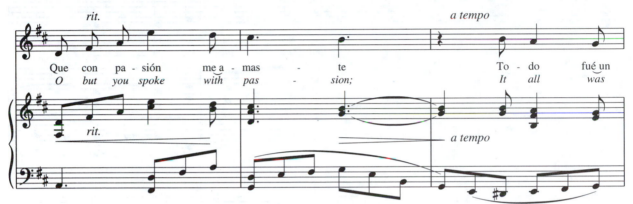

rit.   *a tempo*

Que con pa - sión me a - mas - te To - do fué un
O but you spoke with pas - sion; It all was

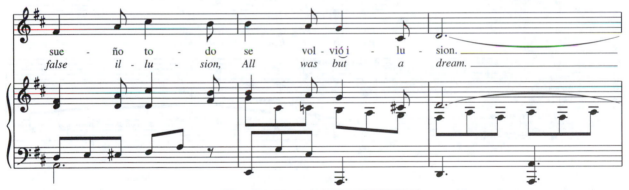

sue - ño to - do se vol - vió i - lu - sion. _____
false il - lu - sion, All was but a dream. _____

1.   2.   *rall.*   *a tempo*

Que mal hi - cis - te _____ con que
You hurt me bad - ly _____ when you

rall.   *a tempo*

me hu - bie - ras a - ma - do, _____ O - fen - dis - te aun
real - ly might have loved me, _____ You slight - ed a

dios Fiel y ver - da - de - ro. _____
god, True and faith - ful ev - er.

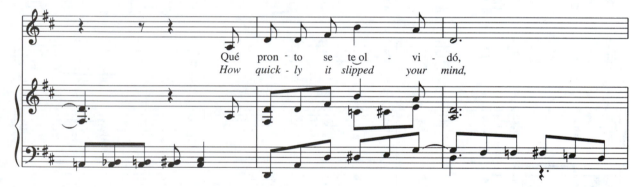

Qué pron - to se te ol - vi - dó,
How quick - ly it slipped your mind,

rall. a tempo

Que fui tu a - mor pri - me - ro, _____ To - do fué un
I was your on - ly lov - er, _____ It all was

sue - ño to - do se vol-vió i - lu - sion. _____
false il - lu - sion, All was but a dream. _____

Se nel ben sempre incostante

(High Voice)

Background and Performance Notes, page 72

Se nel ben sempre incostante	If in time of gladness fickle Fortune
Fortuna vagante,	Is not dependable,
Di farsi stabile uso non ha,	As she is not used to constancy,
Anco mutabile nel mal sarà.	She may also be changeable in time of sorrow.

Reprinted from the International Music Co. collection entitled
Italian Songs of the Seventeenth and Eighteenth Centuries, Volume 2.

278

sta - bi - le u - so non ha, di far - si sta - bi - le

sf

sostenendo il canto

u - so non ha, _____ u - so non ha, An - co mu - ta - bi - le, an - co mu-

ta - bi - le nel__ mal sa - rà, nel mal sa - rà, nel mal sa - rà,

marc.

an - co mu - ta - bi - le, mu - ta - bi - le nel mal sa - rà, _____

an - co mu - ta - bi - le __ nel __ mal sa - rà.

Realization by
Luigi Dallapiccola

Se nel ben sempre incostante

(Low Voice)

Music by
Alessandro Stradella
(1645–1682)

Background and Performance Notes, page 72

Se nel ben sempre incostante
Fortuna vagante,
Di farsi stabile uso non ha,
Anco mutabile nel mal sarà.

If in time of gladness fickle Fortune
Is not dependable,
As she is not used to constancy,
She may also be changeable in time of sorrow.

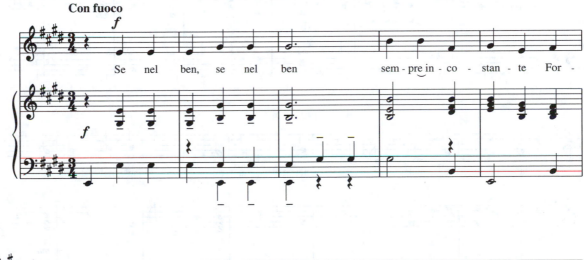

Reprinted from the International Music Co. collection entitled
Italian Songs of the Seventeenth and Eighteenth Centuries, Volume 2.

sta - bi - le u - so non ha, di far - si sta - bi - le

sostenendo il canto

u - so non ha, _____ u - so non ha, An - co mu - ta - bi - le, an - co mu-

ta - bi - le nel mal sa - rà, nel mal sa - rà, nel mal sa - rà,

marc.

an - co mu - ta - bi - le, mu - ta - bi - le nel mal sa - rà, _____

an - co mu - ta - bi - le __ nel __ mal sa - rà.

283

Think on Me

(High Voice)

Alicia Ann Scott
(1810–1900)/
Mary, Queen of Scots
Arranged by
Richard D. Row

Background and Performance Notes, page 72

eyes are bright - est, when griefs are slight - est
woes are nigh thee, when. friends all fly thee,
plea - sure fly - ing, when hope is dy - ing,

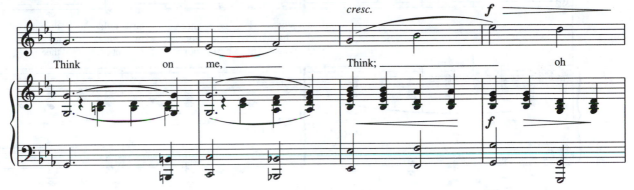

cresc. *f*

Think on me, _____ Think; _____ oh

f

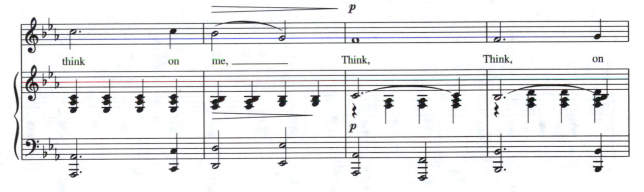

p

think on me, _____ Think, Think, on

p

1 - 2. 3.

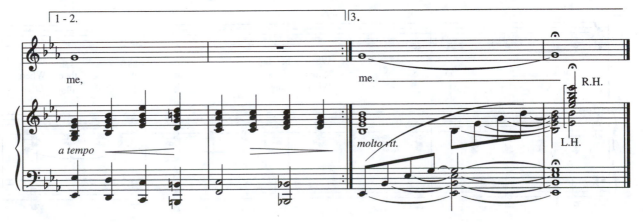

me, me. _____

a tempo *molto rit.* R.H.

L.H.

Think on Me

(Low Voice)

Alicia Ann Scott
(1810–1900)/
Mary, Queen of Scots
Arranged by
Richard D. Row

Background and Performance Notes, page 72

1. When I no more be-hold thee
2. In all Thine hours of glad-ness,
3. When Thou hast none to cheer thee

Think _____ on me,

By all Thine eyes have told me,
If e'er I soothed thy sad-ness,
When no fond heart is near thee

Think _____ on me.

When hearts are light - est, When
When foes are by thee, When
When lone - ly sigh - ing, O'er

eyes   are bright - est, when griefs   are slight - est
woes   are nigh - thee, when friends all fly - thee,
plea - sure fly - ing, when hope is dy - ing,

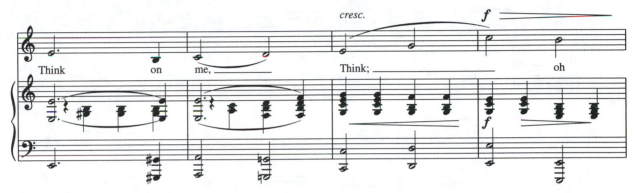

cresc.   *f*

Think   on me,   Think;   oh

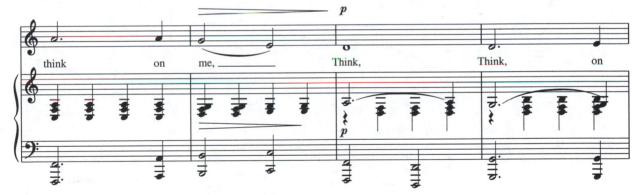

p

think   on me,   Think,   Think, on

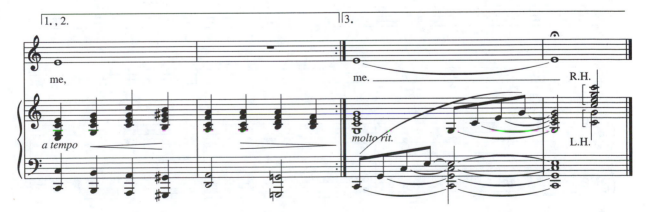

1. , 2.   3.

me,   me.   R.H.

a tempo   *molto rit.*   L.H.

Words by
A. E. Housman

When I was one-and-twenty

Music by
C. Armstrong Gibbs
(1889–1960)

(High Voice)

Background and Performance Notes, page 72

When I was one-and- twen - ty I heard a wise man say "Give crowns and pounds and guin - eas But not your heart a - way; Give pearls a - way and ru - bies, But

keep your fan - cy free." But I was one - and -

twen - ty, No use to talk to me. When __

I was one-and-twen - ty I heard him say a -

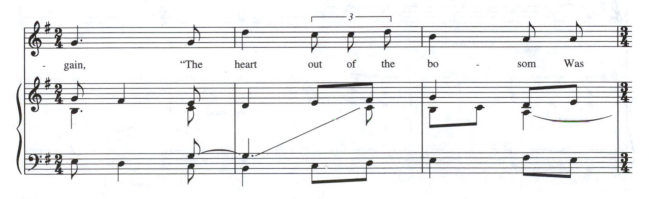

- gain, "The heart out of the bo - som Was

never given in vain; 'Tis

paid with sighs a plen - ty And sold for end - less

rue." And I am two - and -

twen - ty, And oh, 'tis true, 'tis true.

Words by
A. E. Housman

When I was
one-and-twenty

(Low Voice)

Music by
C. Armstrong Gibbs
(1889–1960)

Background and Performance Notes, page 72

keep your fan - cy free." But I was one - and -

twen - ty, No use to talk to me. When __

I was one - and - twen - ty I heard him say a -

gain, "The heart out of the bo - som Was

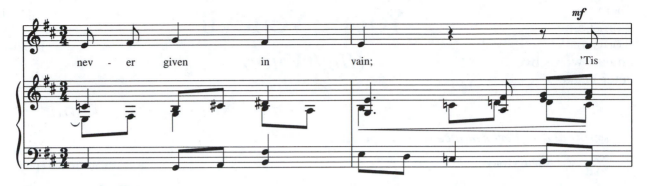

nev - er given in vain; 'Tis

paid with sighs a plen - ty And sold for end - less

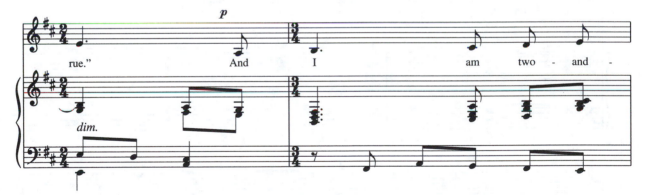

rue." And I am two - and -

twen - ty, And oh, 'tis true, 'tis true.

Poem by
Björnstjerne
Björnson
English words by
Peter Pears

Young Venevil

(High Voice)

Music by
Frederick Delius
(1862–1934)

Background and Performance Notes, page 72

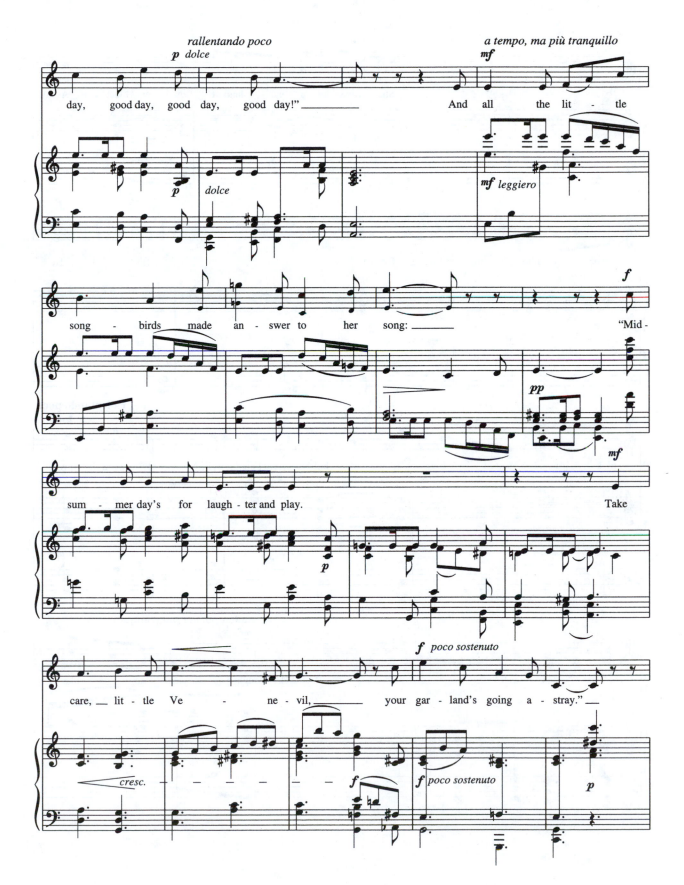

295

light - ning you hear his laugh - ter still: _____

"Mid - sum - mer day's for laugh - ter and play.

Take care, lit - tle Ve - ne - vil, _____ your

poco sostenuto   *a tempo*

gar - land's gone a - stray." _____

Poem by
Björnstjerne
Björnson
English words by
Peter Pears

Young Venevil
(Low Voice)

Music by
Frederick Delius
(1862–1934)

Background and Performance Notes, page 72

Young Ve - ne-vil ran with her heart on fire to her lov - er so dear, to her lov - er so dear.

She sang till she made all the church - bells ring: "Good

day,   good day,   good day,   good day!" _____   And   all   the   lit - tle

song - birds   made   an - swer to   her   song: _____   "Mid -

sum - mer day's   for   laugh - ter and play.   Take

care,   lit - tle   Ve -   ne - vil, _____   your   gar - land's going   a - stray." __

light - ning you hear his laugh - ter still: _____

"Mid - sum - mer day's for laugh - ter and play.

Take care, lit - tle Ve - ne - vil, _____ your

gar - land's gone a - stray." _____

poco sostenuto

a tempo

301

Sample Warm-Up

The following vocalises are included to provide a sample series of effective warm-up exercises (review Chapters 2 and 3). All exercises end on a reasonably low pitch where the vocal folds are most relaxed. These exercises should be sung at only a moderately loud level and, for best results, supervised and adapted by a competent teacher. The goal of these and any other warm-up exercises is to gently stimulate blood flow in the vocal folds to improve and enhance their responsiveness during performance.

1. (Exercise 2.1)

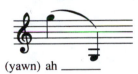

(yawn) ah _____

2. (Exercise 2.2)

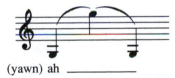

(yawn) ah _____

3. (Exercise 2.3)

ah _____

4. (Exercise 2.4)

ah _____

5. (Exercise 2.9)

ah _____

6. (Exercise 2.10)

ah _____

7. (Exercise 2.12)

ee   ay   ah   oh   oo

8. (Exercise 2.13)

vee _____   vee _____   vee _____   vee

9. (Exercise 3.1)

Hah   Hah   Hah   Hah
(in) (out) (in) (out) (in) (out) (in) (out)

10. (Exercise 3.2)

Hah   Hah   Hah   Hah   Hah

11. (Exercise 3.3)

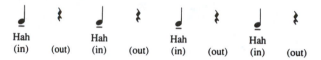

ah

12. (Exercise 3.5)

nah __ nah __ nah __ nah __ nah __ nah __ nah   nah _____

13. (Exercise 3.7)

hah _____

14. (Exercise 3.8)

ah _____

For Further Study

Listed below are several publications that may be used to advance the vocal development of beginning and intermediate voice students. They are also useful in acquainting students with different styles of songs. Certain publications are available in two or more volumes and high and low keys.

Title	Editor or Composer	Publisher
All Sondheim	Sondheim	Warner Bros.
American Folksongs Collection		G. Schirmer
Anthology of French Song	Spicker	G. Schirmer
Ballad Book, The	Niles	Dover
Best of Broadway Today, The		Warner Bros.
Book of Golden Broadway, The		Warner Bros.
Collected Songs	Vaughan Williams	Oxford University Press
Contemporary Theatre Songs		Hal Leonard
Definitive Broadway Collection		Hal Leonard
18th Century Italian Songs	Fuchs	International
15 American Art Songs		G. Schirmer
First Book Series, The	Boytim	Hal Leonard
Folksong Arrangements	Britten	Boosey and Hawkes
45 Arias	Handel	International
42 Folk Songs	Brahms	International
Gershwin on Broadway, 1919–1933	Gershwin	Warner Bros.
Great Broadway Songs		Warner Bros.
Golden Era of Motion Picture Songs and Themes, The		CPP/Belwin
Heritage Songster	Dallin	Wm. C. Brown
Heritage of 20th Century British Song, A		Boosey and Hawkes
Irish Country Songs	Hughes	Boosey and Hawkes
Musical Theatre Classics		Hal Leonard
New Illustrated Disney Songbook, The		Hal Leonard
O Tuneful Voice	Roberts	Oxford University Press
Old American Songs	Copland	Boosey and Hawkes
Purcell/Thirty Songs	Roberts	Oxford University Press
Reliquary of English Song	Potter	G. Schirmer

Title	Editor or Composer	Publisher
Second Book Series, The	Boytim	Hal Leonard
Singer's Musical Theatre Anthology, The	Walters	Hal Leonard
36 Arie di Stile Antico	Donaudy	Ricordi
We Love Movie Themes		Warner Bros.
Wind Beneath My Wings and 24 Contemporary Movie Themes		Warner Bros.

Glossary of Musical Terms and Symbols

The terms listed are used in the songs contained in the anthology of this text.

accel.

Accelerando   Accelerate tempo.

Adagio sostenuto   Slow, sustained tempo.

Allegretto   Tempo between allegro and andante.

Allegro   Lively, rapid.

Allegro maestoso   Rapid but majestic.

Allegro ma non troppo   Lively, but not too rapid.

Amabile   Sweetly.

Andante   Moderate, "walking" speed.

Andante con moto   Slow, with flowing movement.

Andante sostenuto   Slow and sustained.

Andante tranquillo   Slow and peaceful.

Andantino molto cantabile   Rather slow and very songlike.

A tempo   Resume original tempo.

Coda   A "tail," a short passage ending a musical composition.

Colla voce   Follow the voice.

Con fuoco   With fire.

Con grazia   With grace.

Con tenerezza   With tenderness.

Crescendo   Gradually increase volume.

D.C.   **Da capo** Go back to the beginning of the song.

D.S.   **Dal segno** Go back to the sign.

>   **Decrescendo** Gradually decrease volume.

dim.   **Diminuendo** Gradually decrease volume.

      Espressivo Expressively.

⌒   **Fermata** Hold.

      Fine Sing to the end or to the word "Fine."

f   **Forte** Loud.

ff   **Fortissimo** Very loud.

      Grazioso Graceful.

      Interlude Music played between sections of a song or aria.

      Langsam Slow.

      Larghetto Quite slow.

      Largo The slowest tempo marking.

      Legato Connected, smooth.

      Lento Slow.

      Lunga Sustained.

      Meno mosso Not so fast.

      Mezza voce With half the power of the voice.

      Mezzo forte Medium loud.

      Mezzo piano Medium quiet.

      Moderato Moderately fast.

      Molto legato Very smooth.

      Molto semplice Very simply.

      Nicht zu langsam Not too slowly.

      Morendo Dying.

pp   **Pianissimo** Very quiet.

p   **Piano** Quiet.

      Piu animato More animated.

      Piu espressivo More expressively.

Piu mosso   More movement, faster.

Poco   A little.

poco rit.   **Poco ritardando**   Slightly decreasing
                    tempo.

rall.   **Rallentando**   Gradually decreasing tempo.

                 Refrain   A repeated section of music.

                 Risoluto   Resolute, determined.

rit.   **Ritardando**   Gradually decreasing tempo.

rit. essen. assai   **Ritardando essenziale assai**   A significant
                       ritard.

                 Sempre crescendo   Continually increasing
                    volume.

sf   **Sforzando**   Sudden emphasis.

                 Ziemlich langsam   Rather slow.

Glossary of Technical Terms

Anatomy	Study of the structure of the human body.
Angle	Projection formed by two diverging surfaces.
Articulation	Process of pronouncing a sound.
Arytenoid	One of a pair of triangular-shaped cartilages attached to the cricoid cartilage. Posteriorly, the vocal cords are joined to them.
"Break"	An interruption in the normal production of sound, caused by muscle spasm.
Bronchiole	Smallest subdivision of the trachea, through which oxygen passes into the lungs.
Bronchus (bronchi, pl.)	Subdivision of the trachea, one branch penetrating each lung.
Cartilage	Tissue having the capability of developing into bone.
"Chest" Register	Lowest register in the male and female range.
Cochlea	Spiral bony tube, located in the inner ear, containing nerve endings necessary for hearing.
Compression	Outward pushing of the air molecules in the production of sound.
Cricoid	Lower circular cartilage of the larynx.
Diaphragm	Massive, dome-shaped muscle dividing the chest cavity from the abdominal cavity.
Diction	Clarity and distinctness of speech or singing.
Duration	Length of time a sound is heard.
Ear Canal	Tube leading from the outer ear to the eardrum.

Eardrum	Membrane that oscillates at the same frequency with which it is disturbed by air waves.
Epiglottis	Leaf-shaped cartilage that serves as a "lid" to the larynx.
Falsetto	Highest register in the male voice.
Focus	Term borrowed from optics, referring to the clarity of tone.
Fundamental	The perceived pitch of a musical sound. Musical spectra consist of many different frequencies, called overtones.
Glottal Fry	Creaky-sounding extreme low part of the voice.
Hard Palate	Anterior bony portion of the roof of the mouth.
Harmonic	A special class of overtones that are whole-number multiples of the fundamental pitch.
"Head" Register	Highest of the main registers in the female voice, middle register of the male voice.
Inner Ear	Cavity containing structures essential for hearing, primarily the cochlea.
Intensity	"Core" or concentration of sound within a tone, which gives it "carrying power," brilliance.
Intercostal Muscles	Groups of muscles that raise and lower ribs.
Involuntary	Term applied to a muscle that cannot be willfully controlled.
Larynx	Voice box.
Lungs	Pair of membranous sacs located in the chest.
Masseters	"Chewing" muscles.
Membrane	Thin, supple tissue that serves as a covering to structures in the body.
Middle Ear	Portion of the ear containing the ear canal and eardrum.
Middle Register	Middle register in the female voice.
Mucosa	Mucous membrane.

Muscle	Bundle of fibers that can contract and relax, resulting in bodily movement.
Noise	Acoustical term referring to sound that emits uneven sound wave.
Ossicles	Three small bones suspended between the eardrum and oval window.
Oval Window	Membrane in the wall of the cochlea that, when vibrating, sets into motion the fluid in the cochlea.
Partial	In most cases, an alternative term for harmonic.
Physiology	Study of the functions of the parts of the human body.
Pitch	The perceived musical note, determined in part by the number of times a sound wave oscillates the ear drum.
Rarefaction	The bouncing back toward the sound source of the elastic air molecules after they have been compressed.
Register	A series of succeeding vocal sounds of equal quality on a scale that differs from another series of succeeding sounds of equal quality.
Resonance	Intensification and prolongation of sound.
Resonator	Sympathetically vibrating surface or cavity that amplifies and dampens partials.
Soft Palate	Muscular membranous section in the roof of the mouth behind hard palate.
Sonant	Consonant that contains vowel sound.
Sternum	Breastbone.
Surd	Voiceless consonant.
Thorax	Chest.
Thyroarytenoid	A pair of muscles that course from the thyroid to the arytenoid. The vocal cords are part of this group.
Thyroid	Upper V-shaped cartilage of the larynx.
Timbre	*See* tone.

Tone	Timbre, or the identifying quality of a sound. Tone is largely dependent on the overtone content of the sound.
Trachea	Windpipe.
Vocal Cords	A pair of muscular folds that vibrate when air passes through them, thereby producing sound.
Whistle Register	Highest register in the female voice.

International Phonetic Alphabet

Spelling	IPA
pat	æ
pay	e
care	ɛr, er
father	ɑː, ɑ
bib	b
church	tʃ
deed, milled	d
pet	ɛ
bee	i
fife, phase	f
gag	g
hat	h
which	hw (also ʍ)
pit	ɪ
pie, by	aɪ
pier	ɪr, ir
judge	dʒ
kick, cat, pique	k
lid, needle	l, l̩ ['nidl̩]
mum	m
no, sudden	n, n̩ ['sʌdn̩]
thing	ŋ
pot, horrid	ɑ
toe, hoarse	o
caught, paw, for	ɔ
noise	ɔɪ
took	ʊ
boot	u
out	au

Spelling	IPA
pop	p
roar	r
sauce	s
ship, dish	ʃ
tight, stopped	t
thin	θ
this	ð
cut	ʌ
urge, term, firm, word, heard	ɝ, ɛr
valve	v
with	w
yes	j
zebra, xylem	z
vision, pleasure, garage	ʒ
about, item, edible, gallop, circus	ə
butter	ɚ

Foreign

Spelling	IPA
French ami	a
French feu	œ
German schön / *French* tu, *German* über	y
German ich / *Scottish* loch	x
French bon	õ, æ̃, ã, œ̃
French compiègne	ɲ

Bibliography

Backus, John. *The Acoustical Foundation of Music*. New York: W. W. Norton and Co., Inc., 1969.

Bordman, Gerald. *American Musical Theatre: A Chronicle*. New York: Oxford University Press, 1992.

Brodnitz, Friedrich. *Keep Your Voice Healthy* (Second Edition). Waltham, MA: College Hill Press, 1987.

Bunch, Meribeth. *Dynamics of the Singing Voice*. New York: Springer-Verlag, 1993.

Craig, David. *On Singing Onstage*. New York: Schirmer Books, 1978.

Denes, Peter, and Pinson, Elliott. *The Speech Chain*. Short Hills, NJ: Bell Telephone Laboratories, 1963.

Emmons, Shirlee, and Sonntag, Stanley. *The Art of the Song Recital*. New York: Schirmer Books, 1979.

Fields, Victor Alexander. *Foundations of the Singer's Art*. New York: Vantage Press, 1977.

Gänzl, Kurt. *Gänzl's Book of the Broadway Musical. 75 Favorite Shows, from* H. M. S. Pinafore *to* Sunset Boulevard. New York: Schirmer, 1995.

Gray, Henry. *Anatomy, Descriptive and Surgical*. Philadelphia: Running Press, 1974.

Ladefoged, Peter. *Elements of Acoustic Phonetics*. Chicago: The University of Chicago Press, 1962.

Large, John. *Contributions of Voice Research to Singing*. San Diego: College Hill Press, 1980.

Large, John. *Vocal Registers in Singing*. Paris: Mouton, 1973.

McGaw, Charles. *Acting Is Believing*. New York: Holt, Rinehart and Winston, 1966.

Miller, Richard. *On the Art of Singing*. New York: Oxford University Press, 1996.

Miller, Richard. *The Structure of Singing*. New York: Schirmer Books, 1986.

Novak, Elaine. *Performing in Musicals*. New York: Schirmer Books, 1988.

Sadie, Stanley, ed. *The New Grove Dictionary of Music and Musicians.* 20 volumes. New York: Macmillan, 1980.

Sataloff, Robert. *Voice: The Science and Art of Clinical Care.* New York: Raven Press, 1991.

Sataloff, Robert, and Ingo Titze. *Vocal Health and Science.* Jacksonville, FL: The National Association of Teachers of Singing, 1991.

Saunders, William H. *The Larynx.* Summit, NJ: CIBA Corporation, 1964.

Silver, Fred. *Auditioning for Musical Theatre.* New York: Newmarket Press, 1985.

Titze, Ingo. *Principles of Voice Production.* New York: Allyn and Bacon, 1994.

Vennard, William. *Developing Voices.* New York: Carl Fischer, Inc., 1973.

Vennard, William. *Singing, the Mechanism and the Technic.* New York: Carl Fischer, Inc., 1969.

Zemlin, Willard. *Speech and Hearing Science.* Englewood Cliffs, NJ: Prentice-Hall, Inc., 1981.

Index

abdominal muscles, 13–14, 15, 16–18, 21, 29–30, 42
accentuation, 17, 20
accompanists, 20, 40, 42, 46
acoustics, 4, 28, 31–33
acting, 40, 44
    study of, 41
Adam's apple, 6
airstream:
    acceleration of, 11, 29, 30
    compression and rarefaction of, 31
    control of, 6, 12–13
    inhalation and exhalation of, 12–16, 21, 29–30, 31
    wave fronts of, 31
alcohol, 37
anesthetics, local, 37
antacids, 37
antihistamines, 36–37
anti-inflammatory drugs, 36
appearance, 5
    dress and, 42–43, 45
arias, 68
arpeggios, 16
articulation, 21, 25, 27, 28–33
    basic points of, 30–33
art songs, 20, 42, 68–72, 221–301
aspirin, 35–36
audiences, 25–26
    impact on, 4, 31, 40, 42
auditions, 45

belting, 44
birth control pills, 38
blood circulation, 6
blood pressure medication, 38
brain, 31
breathiness, 11, 29–30
breathing, 4, 12–18
    exercises for, 16–18
    marking places for, 21, 26
    physiological process of, 12–16, 21
breath support, 12, 14, 20
bronchi, 12, 13
bronchioles, 12, 13

carbon dioxide, 12
carols, 59
cartilages, 6, 7, 12, 29
cheeks, 28, 29
chemotherapy, 38
chest cavity, 32
    muscles of, 13–14
chest register, 33, 34, 43, 44
choirs, 46
church music, 20, 41
classical music, 4, 19, 41–42. *See also* art songs;
    church music; opera
clavicle, 14

clefs, 46–47
club dates, 43
cocaine, 37
cochlea, 31, 32
colds, 36
compact discs, 20
conductors, 40
consonants, 17, 25, 30, 32
coughing, 37
cysts, 38–39

dance, 40, 41, 45
decongestants, 36
dentists, 35, 38
diaphragm, 13–14
diphthongs, 25, 30
diuretics, 38
drugs, 35–38
    side effects of, 35, 36–37
    social, 37
Dylan, Bob, 58

ear, 3, 4, 31–32
    canal of, 31, 32
    disorders of, 36
    inner, 31, 32
    middle, 31, 32
    outer, 31, 32
    ringing in, 11, 36
eardrum, 31, 32
endotracheal tubes, 38
energy, 4, 26, 40, 44
epiglottis, 6, 7
esophagus, 7
exercise, 39
expression marks, 26, 308–9
eyes, 5

facial muscles, 25, 29
falsetto register, 33, 34, 43
fencing, 40, 41, 42
folk songs, 20, 27, 57–63, 75–138
    American, 57–59, 80–85, 98–100, 104–6, 125–28
    English, 59–60, 86–94, 129–38
    Irish, 60, 100–103
    Italian, 60–61, 122–24
    Jamaican, 61, 75–79
    Peruvian, 61–62, 118–21
    Scottish, 62, 95–97, 107–13
    South African, 63, 115–17

gagging sensation, 9
Guthrie, Woody, 58

halitosis, 38
hands, 5, 16
hard palate, 8